JAPANESE

COOKBOOK FOR BEGINNERS

JAPANESE
COOKBOOK FOR BEGINNERS

Classic and Modern Recipes Made Easy

AZUSA ODA

Photography by Thomas J. Story

callisto
publishing
an imprint of Sourcebooks

Published by Callisto Publishing LLC C/O Sourcebooks LLC

P.O. Box 4410, Naperville, Illinois 60567-4410

(630) 961-3900

callistopublishing.com

Printed and bound in China

OGP 2

For my parents,
Yoko Toyama Besch and Yujiro Oda,
and to Kiyona, Saenah, and Akira

INTRODUCTION

You would think with a grandfather who worked as a French chef in Tokyo and an uncle who built a small chain of restaurants in Hiroshima that my knowledge of cooking was passed down from this family lineage. But the truth is, my food memories, inspiration, and skills come solely from the women in my family. My father's mother, who helped raise me, fed me the food I now associate with comfort. My single mom set a delicious, home-cooked meal on the table each day after working a full-time job with a 70-mile commute. My mom's sister and mother both created beautiful osechi (a special New Year's meal), which I still miss to this day.

Even though I ate Japanese food growing up, cooking it was another story. It wasn't until I married and moved in with my husband and stepdaughter that I considered what it meant to have a home. Cooking and eating together created connection and meaning with my new family, and since Japanese food was my comfort and connection to culture, I was determined to learn how to make it a normal part of our lives.

I know how difficult it can be to acclimate to a new way of cooking. Since some of the ingredients in this book may be hard to find, I suggest alternatives that don't compromise the essence of a dish. You can find traditional Japanese dishes like Mixed-Vegetable Sushi Rice (page 78) and Spinach Dressed with Tofu (page 48), but also more contemporary dishes like Mashed Potato Bake (page 64) and Easy Omelet Rice (page 70).

As happens when trying anything new, I had failures along the way, but my desire to learn buoyed me. After a while, I began to find a rhythm. My hope is that you'll find the same joy in cooking delicious Japanese food in your home as well.

CHAPTER ONE

THE JAPANESE KITCHEN

This chapter will give a general overview of the ingredients, tools, and techniques you might need to cook Japanese food. I hope it will be a helpful resource. There may be a number of items you're unfamiliar with, but my guess is you'll also find a lot of overlap with things you already know and have in your home. The "Japanese kitchen," after all, is not a singular space; it's a place in flux. It contains not one culture, but many cultures, histories, and influences.

Stocking Your Kitchen

The evolving, fluctuating nature of food and of cultural and regional differences makes it impossible for me to create a single, definitive list of what should reside in your kitchen. What I offer instead is an overview of what I think of as "basic" ingredients based on how I cook Japanese food, what is widely available in the United States, and what would be helpful in making the recipes from this book. This list may feel long, but you should be able to get almost all of these items at any grocery store, and ones that can be a bit harder to find were included for specific reasons.

PRODUCE

Bamboo shoots (takenoko): Bamboo shoots taste best when fresh, but vacuum-packed shoots are more readily available. Canned whole bamboo shoots are also an option, but I don't recommend the kind that are cut into rectangular strips. They are tough and fibrous and not suitable for the preparation methods in this book.

Burdock root (gobō): This skinny root vegetable can grow up to three feet long. It has a woody texture and earthy taste, and it is usually sliced on the bias for simmered recipes or finely julienned for sautéing. Parsnips can be used as a substitute, but decrease the amount of sugar or mirin, if called for.

Daikon radish: Daikon is a long, thick, white Japanese radish. It is crunchy when raw and varies in flavor from sweet to peppery. The leaves are edible and delicious stir-fried or sautéed. When shopping, look for daikon that are firm and not limp or wrinkled. Conventional radishes can be used instead, if necessary.

Garlic: Garlic is used in marinades, stir-fries, and other Asian-influenced and contemporary dishes. It's often used together with ginger.

Ginger: Unlike garlic, ginger is commonly used as an aromatic in traditional Japanese cooking. It can be grated and used in tempura sauce or on cold tofu, or minced or sliced and used in stir-fries and braised dishes.

Japanese eggplant (nasu): The color of Japanese eggplant is a deep purple, almost black. It's thin-skinned, slender, and usually about eight inches long. Choose ones with tight, shiny, unblemished skin.

Japanese sweet potato (satsumaimo): Japanese sweet potatoes are purplish-red on the outside and white on the inside. When cooked, the flesh turns yellow. They are not as watery as American sweet potatoes and are more like regular potatoes in texture. Kabocha squash can be used as a substitute.

Kabocha squash: Kabocha is a winter squash that has a beautifully speckled forest-green skin and brilliant orange flesh. When cooked, it is sweet, rich, and nutty. See page 57 for more information on how to safely prepare kabocha.

Napa cabbage (hakusai): Chinese napa cabbage is oblong, with white and light green or yellow leaves. It's often used in stir-fries, hot pots, and pickles, and as a filling for pot stickers. Green cabbage can be substituted in some recipes.

Yuzu: Among the different varieties of Japanese citrus, yuzu has been gaining popularity in the United States. The fruit is yellow or green and has a bumpy, uneven surface. Yuzu's flavor is similar to that of a lemon but has a faint sweetness. Its juice and zest are used in cooking applications similar to those of a lemon.

MUSHROOMS

While some of the mushrooms listed below may be difficult to find in some grocery stores, fresh oyster and maitake mushrooms are good substitutes for any of the varieties in this list.

Beech (shimeji): Beech mushrooms are sold in a cluster about the size of your hand. They can be found with a brown or white cap. They are also referred to as bunashimeji and bunapi mushrooms.

Enoki: What distinguishes the long, thin, white enoki from other mushrooms is its texture, which can be described as "crunchy." Like beech mushrooms, enoki can be found sold in a cluster.

Shiitake: Shiitake mushrooms are used both fresh and dried in Japanese cuisine. Fresh shiitakes have a flat cap and look like a smaller version of a portobello mushroom. Dried shiitake mushrooms have a strong flavor and can be rehydrated and used to bring a rich, savory flavor to a dish. The flavor of the mushrooms is so intense that the soaking liquid itself becomes a broth you can cook with.

PROTEINS

Seafood: There are many varieties of seafood consumed in Japan, but this list focuses on what is used in this book. **Sardines** and **mackerel** are small, oily fish with dense flesh. They are commonly salted, broiled, or grilled, and then eaten with grated daikon, lemon, and soy sauce, or simmered in a miso-ginger sauce. The recipes in this book use canned varieties, as they are more easily found. **Tuna** is usually eaten raw in Japan, unless it's canned. Its flesh is red or pink, depending on the cut's fattiness. **Salmon** is popular in Japan, just as it is in the United States. It is commonly found in bento lunches or flaked and used in rice balls. **Black cod** is not actually cod, but sablefish. It has a soft, white flesh and a rich, buttery flavor. It's delicious broiled and cooked in hot pots. **Shrimp** is commonly used in Japanese dishes in a variety of ways, both raw in sushi and grilled, fried, and sautéed.

Meat and poultry: Although global markets are changing consumption habits in Japan, **beef** used to be a small part of a larger meal or only eaten on special occasions. **Pork** is used in dishes like fried pork cutlet (tonkatsu) and braised pork belly (buta no kakuni), among others. **Chicken** is enjoyed in many ways—for example, deep-fried (karaage), grilled (yakitori), or simmered with root vegetables (chikuzenni).

Tofu: Tofu is a product made from soybeans that comes in different levels of softness. As a general rule of thumb, soft tofu is used in more delicate dishes and firm tofu is used in stews, since it holds its shape. **Aburaage** is a thin piece of deep-fried tofu with a spongy texture that adds a subtle richness to a dish. When cut in half, the aburaage can be opened to form a pocket. It can be found in the refrigerated or frozen section of some Asian markets or online.

FERMENTED ITEMS

Bonito flakes (katsuobushi): Bonito flakes are made from thinly shaved skipjack tuna that has been dried, fermented, and smoked. They resemble wood shavings and are sold in small packages, to use for garnishing, or large bags. I recommend getting a large bag for making dashi.

Mirin: Mirin is a sweet rice wine used for cooking. Hon mirin is the best choice because it has no added sugar; the sweetness comes from a natural fermentation process. Aji mirin is cheaper but is sweetened, usually with corn syrup.

Miso: Simply put, miso is a fermented paste made from soybeans, salt, and rice koji. There are many different varieties ranging from sweet and light (*shiromiso*, which means "white miso") to dark and rich (*akamiso*, which means "red miso"). I typically use awase miso, which is a mix of both shiromiso and akamiso, for a range of cooking applications. Check the package and buy a miso made with soybeans, salt, and rice koji as an entry point. Get accustomed to its flavor, then try a different variety—such as one made with barley instead of rice, one with just soybeans, or one with a longer fermentation period, for example.

Rice vinegar (osu): Rice vinegar is mild in flavor and is used in dressings and to season rice when making sushi.

ALLERGEN-FREE ALTERNATIVES

Many people have gluten and soy allergies. Luckily, we live in a time when alternatives are abundant, and we can easily work around these restrictions. Here a few easy swaps to make in the recipes that follow.

If you're allergic to gluten:

Tamari can replace soy sauce. If you're allergic to gluten, try gluten-free tamari. As mentioned on page 6, some brands can contain trace amounts of wheat, so be sure to read the label carefully. The word *tamari* comes from the liquid by-product that would puddle when making miso.

Seek out shirataki noodles. Shirataki noodles are made from konnyaku, a Japanese yam. They can absorb sauces and cook for long periods without becoming mushy. They have a texture unlike wheat-based noodles and may take some getting used to.

If you're allergic to soy:

Instead of soy sauce or tamari, use coconut aminos. Coconut aminos are naturally sweet and are soy- and gluten-free. When using, I suggest decreasing the amount of mirin or sugar, if a recipe calls for either of them.

Use miso made from different beans. Miso can be found made from other beans, such as chickpeas, adzuki, and mung beans. The base flavor is different from soybeans, but these are good alternatives.

Sake: Sake is an alcoholic drink described as Japanese rice wine. For cooking purposes, a big bottle of the cheapest sake is sufficient.

Salted plum (umeboshi): Umeboshi is made from small Japanese plums that are salted and preserved. They are often eaten with rice or packed in the center of a rice ball.

Soy sauce and **tamari:** **Soy sauce** is made from soybeans, wheat, brine, and rice koji. Sometimes soy sauce is made from soybean pulp, so look at the ingredient list to ensure it is made from whole soybeans. **Tamari** is similar to soy sauce, but stronger in flavor. While nearly all brands in the United States are gluten-free, be sure to check the label just in case, as on occasion they can contain trace amounts of wheat.

SPICES, FLAVORINGS, AND HERBS

Furikake: Furikake is a topping used to season rice. There are many types, which may contain dried fish, pickled plum, or nori, just to name a few.

Ground white pepper: White pepper is milder than black pepper and is used in dishes like fried rice, ramen, and pot stickers.

Oyster sauce: Oyster sauce is a thick, brown, sweet condiment made from oyster extract, sugar, salt, and a thickener. It is often used in Chinese-influenced dishes.

Sesame oil: Toasted sesame oil is light to dark amber in color and has a nutty flavor. The color of the oil correlates to the degree to which the sesame seeds are roasted.

Shichimi: A topping sprinkled on noodle dishes and rice bowls to awaken and enhance the flavors, *shichimi* translates to "seven flavors." It can be made up of a different combination of ingredients, such as red chiles, roasted orange peel, sesame seeds, hemp seeds, ground ginger, seaweed, and poppy seeds.

Shiso: Shiso is a Japanese herb that adds brightness to any dish. The aromatics are located on the back of the leaf, so when washing and drying, pat gently so they are not rubbed off. The flavor is unique, but a mixture of basil and mint leaves can be substituted if you can't find shiso.

Wasabi: Wasabi is a green Japanese horseradish, often grated and eaten with sushi. In the United States, it is commonly sold in a tube or in powdered form. To use, the powder is reconstituted with water to form a paste.

Worcestershire sauce: Worcestershire sauce and its offshoots (ustah, chuno, and tonkatsu sauce) are widely used in Japanese cooking.

DRY GOODS

Panko: Panko are dried Japanese breadcrumbs. They're used in fried foods or soaked in milk and used to make tender hamburger steak.

Potato starch (katakuriko): Potato starch is a white powder that is used to thicken sauces and coat ingredients before cooking. Cornstarch can be used as a substitute in most recipes.

Rice: Japanese short-grain rice, sometimes called sushi rice, is standard fare. The grains stick together and are starchier than long- or medium-grain rice. While white rice is more common, short-grain brown rice can also be used.

Sesame seeds: All forms of sesame seeds, both white and black, are used in Japanese cooking—whole seeds, ground seeds, and sesame paste.

Seaweed: There are many forms of seaweed, but the three used in this book are wakame, kombu, and nori. Dried **wakame** is a soft seaweed often used in soups and salads. It dramatically increases in volume when rehydrated. **Kombu** is dried sea kelp that along with bonito flakes and dried shiitake makes the foundational broth used in many dishes. Japanese **nori** comes in a package of large sheets. It is often used as a garnish, as wrappers for rice balls, or in sushi dishes.

JAPANESE NORI

Japanese nori (dried seaweed) has many uses, from using slivers of it to top cold soba to cooking it down to a paste called nori no tsukudani. It's probably best known for wrapping rice balls or for its use in sushi.

After the devastating 2011 Tōhoku earthquake, concerns about radiation in food products from the Fukushima area led to testing and regulation. Compared to Japan, the US regulations are lower when importing Japanese nori because it is assumed to be eaten less regularly in the American diet. I look for nori that comes from the Ariake Sea or the Seto Inland Sea in southern Japan. It is considered a safer premium product and is more expensive, but since we eat it frequently, I believe it is worth paying extra for. Be aware that some brands label their product as "Ariake Nori" but it is not from that region.

NOODLES AND DUMPLING WRAPPERS

Pot sticker wrappers: Pot sticker wrappers come in a vacuum-packed stack and are sold refrigerated or frozen.

Ramen: Ramen is a wheat noodle with a firm, sometimes springy texture. You can find ramen noodles dried and sometimes in the refrigerated or frozen sections.

Soba: Soba is a thin noodle made of buckwheat or a mix of buckwheat and wheat flour. Soba can be eaten with a broth, hot or cold, or dressed like a salad with vegetables. It is sold dried.

Udon: Udon is a thick wheat noodle eaten hot or cold with a dashi-based broth. Sometimes it is panfried with vegetables. You can find udon noodles dried and sometimes in the refrigerated or frozen sections.

Yakisoba: Yakisoba is a soft wheat noodle that is sold in vacuum-packed packages in the refrigerated section. The packaged noodles come steam-cooked and don't require a long cooking time.

Tools and Utensils

I do my best to only buy kitchen gear that is essential or has multiple uses. The following are what I consider the must-have tools and utensils to cook Japanese food at home. While I've included some Japanese-specific utensils, I've noted easy substitutions you probably already have in your kitchen, when possible.

MUST-HAVES

Ceramic grater (oroshiki): A round ceramic grater is useful when grating ginger or daikon. There is a trough in the outer ring that collects the pulp and juices. A Microplane grater is a good substitute.

Drop-lid (otoshibuta): A drop-lid is often used in simmered dishes to prevent too much liquid from evaporating, allowing the ingredients to cook more evenly. As a substitute, a piece of aluminum foil can be pressed down into the pot.

Nonstick pan: A nonstick pan, preferably ceramic, is useful for making rolled egg omelets and for cooking pot stickers.

Pot with a tight-fitting lid: To cook perfect rice, all you need is a pot with a lid. The trick is to make sure the lid fits tightly so it completely traps the moisture and heat while cooking.

Sharp knife: You don't need a fancy Japanese knife for these recipes, just a sharp one. It's essential when thinly slicing meat or fish, and is much safer than a dull knife.

Steamer basket: An expandable metal steamer basket is ideal for cooking vegetables. You use less water, compared to boiling, and have the added benefit of maintaining more of the vegetable's nutrients.

Fine-mesh strainer: A couple of fine-mesh strainers in different sizes, including a small ladle-like one sometimes called a skimmer or a spider, are useful for draining rice and vegetables and straining dashi. Colanders lined with paper towels can work in a pinch, but they don't always prevent the rice grains from slipping through and the drainage isn't as good.

NICE-TO-HAVES

Ceramic pot (donabe): A donabe retains heat well and has many uses. As with a conventional pot, you can use it to cook rice, make hot pots, steam vegetables, and make porridge and soup.

Chopsticks (ohashi, saibashi): Ohashi is the standard utensil for eating at every meal. See "The Etiquette of Chopsticks" on page 113 for more information. Saibashi are chopsticks made specifically for cooking. They are longer than ones used for eating, to prevent your hands from getting burned when cooking over the stove.

Japanese mortar and pestle (suribachi, surikogi): The Japanese mortar and pestle is designed to be relatively lightweight and efficient in grinding down sesame seeds and nuts to make pastes and dressings. A coffee or spice grinder can be used as a substitute. See page 10 for more detailed information.

Kitchen scale: There are some ingredients, like bonito flakes, that are easier to measure using a kitchen scale. A scale also allows for more accurate measurements than measuring cups.

Rice paddle (shamoji): A shamoji is the best tool to fluff cooked rice and mix ingredients into it. It is designed to scoop the rice without smashing the grains. Wet the paddle before using to prevent the rice from sticking to it. A silicone spatula is a good substitute for mixing, and a fork can work for fluffing.

SURIBACHI AND SURIKOGI

A suribachi and surikogi is the equivalent of a mortar and pestle and is used for grinding ingredients such as sesame seeds. However, instead of pounding, the mortar has grooves that line the interior of the bowl and the pestle moves across them to grind the ingredients. It is a gentle motion that is ergonomically designed and fun to use, once you get the hang of it. Although I suggest a coffee or spice grinder in its place, a suribachi and surikogi use a gentler method of pressing the seeds and extracting the oils.

To use this tool, first place a small, damp towel underneath the suribachi to prevent it from slipping. Hold the surikogi inside the bowl with your dominant hand a third of the way up from the bottom. Rest the palm of your other hand on top of the surikogi. While you move your dominant hand in a circular motion around the bowl, use your secondary hand to gently press down on the surikogi. The fulcrum should be at the top of the surikogi and your secondary hand.

By simultaneously applying light pressure down and around, you can exert less effort when grinding. It takes some practice, but it allows you to have more control over the level of grinding. The process can be satisfying and meditative, so if you enjoy cooking, this is a tool that will allow you to watch an ingredient transform before your eyes.

Serving dishes: Different bowls and dishes are used depending on the food being served. These are some of the more commonly used ones. A **rice bowl (ochawan)** is made of ceramic and is small enough to fit in one hand. A **miso soup bowl (owan)** is similar in size but is typically made from wood or lacquered wood and has a more rounded bottom. A **donburi** is a large ceramic bowl that is used for rice bowl dishes and hot udon or soba. A ramen donburi is similar in size but has a wider lip and is more angular.

During a meal, if there are a variety of communal dishes, a **torizara** is provided. A torizara is a medium-sized individual plate to place communal food on and eat from. **Small bowls (kobachi)** are used for sauces like tempura dipping sauce, ponzu, etc. **Small plates (kozara)** are used for soy sauce when eating pot stickers or sushi. While these are standard in a Japanese household, please don't feel daunted by this list—use the dishware you currently have. The food will taste just as good.

Preparation and Cooking Techniques

Many of the following methods are common, useful cooking preparations regardless of whether you're cooking Japanese food. This is not a comprehensive list, but an idea of what you can expect to find used in this book.

Braising (itameni): When braising, an ingredient is first seared, then simmered in a sauce for a long time. Cooking over high heat first seals in juices and prevents ingredients from breaking down quickly.

Broiling (yaku): This form of high-heat cooking is faster than roasting and gives a nice blister and char.

Deep-frying (ageru): Deep-frying requires food to be submerged in an oil that can withstand temperatures of at least 350°F. This includes avocado oil, rice bran oil, coconut oil, and animal fat.

OIL TEMPERATURE TESTS

It's crucial to pay attention to the temperature of the oil when deep- or shallow-frying. Make sure you heat the oil slowly over medium heat or lower, then adjust the heat gradually during cooking, if necessary. Extreme heat will make the oil unstable, so it's important to be patient and refrain from making drastic heat adjustments.

One of the hardest things to know is when the oil is ready or if it is too hot, especially without a thermometer. If the oil is smoking, or if the food you're cooking browns before the inside is cooked, the oil is too hot. Here are two of my tried-and-true ways for checking if oil is ready for frying:

The Chopstick Technique: Touch your wooden chopsticks to the bottom of the pot of oil. If small bubbles rise enthusiastically, the oil is ready for frying.

The Batter Technique: Drop a little batter or panko (or whatever you're frying) into the pot. If it sinks to the bottom or bubbles timidly, the oil is not hot enough. If it bubbles enthusiastically, the oil is ready.

Dry-frying/pan-roasting (iru): This method requires constant stirring or shaking of the pan. The goal is to wick away the moisture in order to dry out or toast the ingredients, which can range from sesame seeds to fish or eggs.

Grinding (suru): Grinding breaks down ingredients into smaller pieces; with seeds and nuts, it releases the oils and flavors.

Simmering (niru): Simmering is a gentle method of cooking where long, even cooking is desired. Dishes like miso soup and hot pots start with dashi and are brought to a boil before simmering the ingredients in the broth.

Steeping (hitasu): Steeping allows an ingredient to infuse the liquid it's sitting in with its flavor. The liquid can be hot or cold and the time frame can range from 10 minutes to a week or more.

Stir-frying (itameru): Stir-frying is done over medium-high to high heat. The process is faster than sautéing and results in vegetables that are tender-crisp.

How to Use This Book

My goal is for you to find cooking Japanese food to be practical and delicious. I know how intimidating it can be when you begin to explore another cuisine, so I simplified the ingredients and methods as much as possible, without losing the spirit of each dish. I hope this makes the recipes feel approachable and entirely possible in your home kitchen.

Most of the dishes are ones I hope you'll make on a weekday or any day. Where possible, I provided ingredient substitutions that are common in a conventional American grocery store, but some ingredients, like bonito flakes and kombu, are essential to Japanese cuisine, and I feel they are worth seeking out at an Asian market or online.

In chapter 2, you will find the staple recipes that make up the foundation of Japanese cooking, like how to cook rice or make dashi. Many of the recipes following that chapter will draw upon these foundational recipes.

I should also mention that most of these dishes are to be enjoyed with rice. Unless you are making a noodle dish like udon or ramen or a rice dish like fried rice or omuraisu, steamed rice is considered a staple and should accompany all Japanese meals.

LABELS

Each recipe is tagged with labels meant to help easily identify the dish for people with certain food intolerances or allergies, diet or lifestyle choices, and busy schedules. The label categories are: Freezer Friendly, Gluten-Free, Nut-Free, One Pot, 30 Minutes or Less, Vegan, and Vegetarian.

A note about the Gluten-Free label: Soy sauce contains gluten. As someone with a gluten intolerance, I know how challenging it is to have this restriction. Since gluten-free tamari is interchangeable with soy sauce, all recipes with soy sauce as its only gluten-containing ingredient have tamari listed as well and are labeled Gluten-Free. **Be sure to use gluten-free tamari if you have a gluten intolerance.**

A note about the Vegetarian and/or Vegan label: When a recipe's only nonvegan or nonvegetarian ingredient is dashi made with bonito flakes, I've labeled the recipe as Vegan or Vegetarian (depending on the recipe) and have listed the Vegan Dashi as an option in the ingredients list.

TIPS

The tips featured in the recipes will help guide you and give context to the cooking process:

Cooking Tip: How to get the most out of cooking a particular dish.

Ingredient Tip: How to buy, use, or store a particular ingredient.

Prep Tip: How to prepare a recipe more efficiently.

Variation Tip: How to add or substitute ingredients to make things easier or change things up.

CHAPTER TWO

STAPLES

BASIC SHORT-GRAIN RICE

Gluten-Free, Nut-Free, One Pot, Vegan

PREP TIME: 45 MINUTES, INCLUDING SOAKING TIME **|** COOK TIME: 30 MINUTES **|** SERVES 4

Rice that's cooked properly has a glossy sheen. When you eat it, you should be able to detect each grain and there should be a slight bite to it. A pot with a tight-fitting lid is essential for this recipe because the seal traps the moisture and heat. If there is a small leak, the rice will not cook evenly, leaving some grains at the top uncooked. What I've described below is not the traditional way of washing rice, but a method I find easier to do with the same results.

1½ cups short-grain
  white rice

1½ cups, plus
  2 tablespoons,
  filtered water

TO PREPARE THE RICE:

1. Put the rice in a small pot and add enough cold water to cover the rice. Grab a handful of grains in one hand and gently rub them together under the water. Do this a few times. The water will become cloudy.

2. Slowly tip out the cloudy water without discarding any of the rice. You don't have to drain the water completely.

3. With your hand shaped loosely like a claw, put your hand in the pot with the wet rice and rotate your hand at your wrist in a circular motion. You should be agitating the grains with your knuckles. Quickly rotate your hand inside the pot this way approximately 30 times.

4. Place the pot under a faucet and turn on the cold water in a slow stream. As the pot fills with water, grab a handful of grains and in one hand and gently rub them together as before. Turn off the water when the rice is covered by an inch. Slowly drain the water by tipping the pot again.

5. Repeat steps 3 and 4 once or twice more, until the water is somewhat clear and most of the starch has been washed off. When you're finished washing, drain the rice in a fine-mesh strainer for 15 minutes.

6. Put the drained rice back in the pot and add the filtered water. Cover and let it soak for 20 minutes.

TO COOK THE RICE:

1. Uncover the pot and place it over medium heat. Bring the water to a boil and put the lid back on. Turn the heat down to low and cook for 20 minutes. Do not lift the lid.

2. Turn off the heat and let the rice steam for an additional 10 minutes. Do not lift the lid.

3. Wet a rice paddle or fork with water and gently fold the rice to fluff.

> **COOKING TIP:** White rice can be cooked in an electric pressure cooker using a 1:1 rice to water ratio. Set your appliance to manual high pressure for 3 minutes and allow the pressure to release naturally once cooking has ended.

RICE TROUBLESHOOTING

Though seemingly simple, making rice can be intimidating. Here are some things that might help:

- A pot with a tight-fitting lid is essential.
- Based on the amount of rice you're cooking, the size of your pot matters. A 1½-quart pot can cook ¾ to 1½ cups (2 to 4 servings) of rice. A 2-quart pot can cook 1½ to 2¼ cups (4 to 6 servings) of rice.
- Remember that different varieties of rice require different amounts of water. There may be some trial and error necessary. For example, if your rice comes out too dry, add 1 or 2 tablespoons more water the next time you cook a pot. Conversely, if the rice is mushy, decrease the amount of water by 1 or 2 tablespoons.
- Although washing the rice is necessary, if you are pressed for time, drain as much water as you can after washing, then decrease the amount of water you add to the pot by 1 tablespoon. Skip the soaking and set to cook.

BASIC DASHI

Freezer Friendly, Gluten-Free, Nut-Free, One Pot, 30 Minutes or Less

PREP TIME: 5 MINUTES | COOK TIME: 15 MINUTES | MAKES ABOUT 3½ CUPS

The foundation of many Japanese dishes is a broth called dashi. Among the different types of dashi, this one—made with kombu and bonito flakes—is the most common. Compared to making chicken stock or broth, dashi is a breeze. I suggest initially measuring out the ingredients to familiarize yourself with the proportions, but the recipe is forgiving. If you'd like, double the batch and freeze for a later use. To freeze, pour the dashi into an airtight container and freeze for up to 6 months. Defrost overnight, or gently in a pot over medium-low heat.

---

2 (7-inch) pieces kombu

4¼ cups filtered water

3 to 4 loosely packed
cups bonito flakes

1. In a large pot, combine the kombu and water and cover the pot. Turn the heat to medium. When the water starts to boil, uncover the pot and remove and discard the kombu. Leave the lid off.

2. When the water comes to a rolling boil, add the bonito flakes. Turn the heat off immediately, cover, and let sit for 10 minutes.

3. Place a fine-mesh strainer in a larger bowl and line it with a cheesecloth or paper towel. Carefully pour the dashi through the strainer and into the bowl. Press lightly to squeeze out any remaining liquid.

INGREDIENT TIP: Save the soaked bonito flakes to make Bonito Rice Topping (page 24).

VARIATION TIP: Instant dashi comes as a powder you dissolve in hot water or as a small tea bag–like pouch you can steep. If you use instant dashi, decrease the amount of salt, soy sauce, and/or miso in a recipe, since salt is usually added, and check for recognizable ingredients, as most brands have additives.

VEGAN DASHI

Gluten-Free, Nut-Free, One Pot, Vegan

PREP TIME: 5 MINUTES | SOAK TIME: 1 HOUR | COOK TIME: 25 MINUTES | MAKES ABOUT 4 CUPS

The Basic Dashi (page 18) is made with bonito flakes and kombu, but this one uses kombu and dried shiitake mushrooms to make a wonderful alternative for those who are vegan or vegetarian. The broth is rich and hearty and the kombu and shiitake complement each other well.

6 small dried shiitake mushrooms

2 (7-inch) pieces kombu

4¼ cups filtered water

1. Combine the shiitake, kombu, and water in a medium pot and cover the pot. Let the mixture sit for 1 hour.

2. Turn the heat to medium-low and slowly bring the mixture to a boil. Uncover and remove and discard the kombu. Continue to simmer the shiitake, uncovered, for 10 minutes.

3. Place a fine-mesh strainer in a larger bowl and line it with a cheesecloth or paper towel. Remove and discard the shiitake and carefully pour the dashi through the strainer and into the bowl. Press lightly to squeeze out any remaining liquid.

PREP TIP: You can skip the cooking step entirely: Put the shiitake, kombu, and water in a container and let it sit overnight in the refrigerator. When you're ready to use, strain the dashi through a fine-mesh strainer lined with a cheesecloth or paper towel and press lightly to squeeze out any remaining liquid.

Misoshiru

MISO SOUP

Gluten-Free, Nut-Free, One Pot, 30 Minutes or Less, Vegan

PREP TIME: 10 MINUTES | COOK TIME: 15 MINUTES | SERVES 4

To me, miso soup is soothing and centering. My grandmother would add different kinds of vegetables, and even fish, making it a hearty, healthy soup. I suggest experimenting by adding three or so ingredients at a time. Some of my favorite additions are Japanese sweet potato, enoki mushrooms, beech mushrooms, green cabbage, daikon radish, potatoes, carrots, aburaage, and kabocha squash. Pay attention to how the different ingredients work together and change the flavor of the soup and create your favorite combinations. You can use whatever kind of miso you prefer. As a general rule of thumb, white miso is less salty and red miso is richer and saltier. Use the amounts listed here as a guide and be sure to taste and adjust accordingly.

3 small pinches dried wakame

2½ cups Basic Dashi (page 18) or Vegan Dashi (page 19)

¼ onion, sliced

¼ (14-ounce) package soft tofu, cut into small cubes

1 tablespoon miso, plus more as needed

1 scallion, white and green parts, chopped, for garnish

1. Put the wakame in a small bowl, amply cover with water, and set aside.

2. Warm the dashi in a pot over medium heat. When it comes to a boil, add the onions and tofu and lower the heat to medium-low. Cook until the onions are soft, 5 to 7 minutes.

3. Transfer a few tablespoons of dashi to a small bowl and add the miso. Whisk to dissolve, then pour the mixture back into the pot. Stir and taste the soup, then add more miso if needed, until you reach your desired level of saltiness.

4. Squeeze the rehydrated wakame to remove the excess water, then add it to the pot. Stir to combine and let sit for a couple minutes to warm through.

5. Serve in individual bowls, topped with the scallion.

> **COOKING TIP:** Once you add the miso paste to the pot, keep it at a low heat. If the soup boils, it will change the flavor and kill any beneficial probiotic strains.

Kinokojiru

CLEAR MUSHROOM SOUP

Gluten-Free, Nut-Free, One Pot, 30 Minutes or Less, Vegan

PREP TIME: 10 MINUTES | COOK TIME: 10 MINUTES | SERVES 4

This mushroom soup belongs to a family of soups called sumashijiru. Sumashijiru are clear, clean-tasting soups, often made with just a few seasonal ingredients. With the soup's pure taste, it works well with many dishes, but I like it with sushi rice–based ones, like Mixed-Vegetable Sushi Rice (page 78), Football Sushi (page 76), and Tuna Chirashi with Snow Peas (page 80). Feel free to use oyster mushrooms instead of beech mushrooms if you can't find them.

1 piece aburaage

3¼ cups Basic Dashi (page 18) or Vegan Dashi (page 19)

4 fresh shiitake mushrooms, stemmed and thinly sliced

1 (3.5-ounce) package beech mushrooms, trimmed and separated by hand

1 tablespoon sake

1 tablespoon soy sauce or tamari

1½ teaspoons mirin

Pinch salt

1. Fold a paper towel in half and place the aburaage inside. Press with a rolling pin to release any excess oil. Cut the aburaage in half, then slice each half crosswise into medium strips.

2. Heat the dashi and aburaage in a medium pot over medium-high heat. Once it comes to a boil, add the shiitake and beech mushrooms.

3. Add the sake, soy sauce, mirin, and salt. Taste and adjust the seasonings accordingly. Bring to a boil and serve.

VARIATION TIP: Because this is a seasonal dish, you can vary the ingredients based on what looks good at the market. Spinach, carrots, tofu, snow peas, daikon, chicken, and shrimp are just a few examples. Only a few ingredients should be in the soup at a time, and they should not be crowded. For New Year's Day, a type of sumashijiru called ozōni is served with mochi in the soup.

Tamagoyaki

ROLLED EGG OMELET

Gluten-Free, Nut-Free, 30 Minutes or Less, Vegetarian

PREP TIME: 5 MINUTES | COOK TIME: 10 MINUTES | SERVES 4

Sweetened egg omelets are perfect for bento lunches or picnics because they're sturdy and keep well. They are a good counterpoint to Japanese "Fried" Chicken (page 118) or to include in your DIY Hand Roll Sushi (page 104) night. The method will take some practice, so if it doesn't go right, don't be discouraged. I once made it and it took on the shape of a triangle. I shrugged it off—it tastes just the same. I recommend watching a video first to get a feel for the technique before diving in.

1 teaspoon olive oil

3 large eggs

1½ teaspoons sugar

½ teaspoon mirin

¼ teaspoon soy sauce or tamari

Pinch salt

TO PREPARE THE EGGS:

1. Heat the oil in a small nonstick pan over medium-low heat.

2. Combine the eggs, sugar, mirin, soy sauce, and salt in a small bowl. Mix without creating air bubbles by whisking with a pair of chopsticks or a fork while keeping the tips touching the bottom of the bowl. Whisk until the whites have broken and are incorporated into the yolk.

3. Wipe the excess oil from the pan with a paper towel and set the paper towel aside. Test the heat of the pan by dripping a little egg on it. If it sizzles, the pan is ready.

TO MAKE THE OMELET:

1. Pour in enough egg to thinly cover the bottom of the pan. Swirl the egg around to evenly coat and let it cook.

2. When the edges look dry and the egg has set but is still glossy, about 1 minute, use a pair of chopsticks or a spatula to quickly go around the edges to loosen the egg.

3. Starting on one side, roll the egg onto itself an inch or so at a time. The egg should look like a thick rectangle. Once the egg has been rolled to the opposite side of the pan, use the paper towel you set aside earlier to rub a little oil onto the pan.

4. With the rolled egg still to one side, add another thin layer of egg to the pan and swirl to coat evenly. The raw egg will come to the edge of the cooked egg.

5. Lift the cooked egg to let some raw egg seep underneath. This will help connect the two layers.

6. Once again, when the raw egg looks cooked around the edges but the center is still glossy, begin to roll the egg onto itself, this time starting with the rolled egg.

7. When this layer is rolled onto itself and the rectangle has increased in thickness, use the paper towel again to wipe on more oil, and repeat the rolling process, always starting with the cooked omelet, until all of the egg mixture has been used.

8. The finished omelet should be in the shape of a brick. Reduce the heat to low and turn the egg to cook on each of the four sides until firm.

9. Remove the pan from the heat. Cool for a few minutes, then slice the omelet into 8 pieces and serve.

VARIATION TIP: Because the flavor is sweet, egg omelets are a good vehicle for vegetables. For example, try whisking in chopped steamed spinach, but make sure to squeeze out excess moisture first.

Katsuo Denbu

BONITO RICE TOPPING

Freezer Friendly, Gluten-Free, Nut-Free, One Pot, 30 Minutes or Less

PREP TIME: 5 MINUTES | COOK TIME: 20 MINUTES | MAKES ABOUT ½ CUP

I'm embarrassed to say that for years I threw away the bonito flakes after making dashi and I was riddled with guilt every time. Cooking the leftover bonito flakes gives it a second life. You can also make this with fresh bonito flakes, if you wish— just note it will take less time to crisp up on the stove. Use this as a topping for rice or mix it in cooked rice to make Bonito Rice Balls (page 44). You can freeze it if you feel you won't be able to consume it within 10 days.

Leftover bonito flakes
   from making 1 recipe
   Basic Dashi (page 18),
   or 3 to 4 cups loosely
   packed store-bought
   bonito flakes

3 tablespoons water

1 tablespoon soy sauce
   or tamari

2 teaspoons sugar

2 teaspoons mirin

2 teaspoons
   sesame seeds

1. Put the bonito flakes in a small, dry skillet and cook, stirring constantly over medium-low heat until the flakes are dry and crisp, about 6 minutes. Be careful not to burn them. Turn off the heat and let the flakes sit for 5 minutes to cool.

2. With your fingers, massage the flakes in the pan until they break up and become powdery. A few larger pieces are okay.

3. Add the water, soy sauce, sugar, and mirin to the pan and bring to a boil over medium heat. Turn the heat down to medium-low and cook, stirring constantly, until the moisture has cooked off and the flakes are dry, about 6 minutes.

4. Stir in the sesame seeds. Let the mixture cool, then store in a container in the refrigerator for up to 10 days.

Dashijōyu

DASHI SOY SAUCE

Gluten-Free, Nut-Free, One Pot, 30 Minutes or Less

PREP TIME: 10 MINUTES **|** COOK TIME: 10 MINUTES, PLUS 1 HOUR TO COOL **|** MAKES ABOUT ½ CUP

Dashi soy sauce can be used in place of regular soy sauce wherever it's used as a seasoning at the table. For example, you can drizzle it over a simple bowl of rice and eggs or use it in the recipes for Cold Tofu, Three Ways (page 50) and Sushi Bowls (page 103).

½ cup soy sauce or tamari

1¼ tablespoons mirin

2½ teaspoons sake

1 loosely packed cup bonito flakes

1. Combine the soy sauce, mirin, and sake in a small pot and bring to a boil over medium heat. Immediately turn the heat to low and add the bonito flakes. Cook for 3 minutes.

2. Remove the pot from the heat and let cool for 1 hour.

3. Pour the mixture through a fine-mesh strainer into a mason jar or other container with a tight-fitting lid. Press to squeeze out the liquid from the bonito flakes and discard the flakes.

4. Cover the jar tightly and store in the refrigerator for up to 3 months.

Ponzu

CITRUS SOY SAUCE

Gluten-Free, Nut-Free

PREP TIME: 10 MINUTES **|** STEEP TIME: 2 DAYS **|** MAKES 1¼ CUPS

Ponzu is salty and tart. It goes well with meat dishes such as Hamburger Steak (page 112) because it cuts through the richness, and it adds a bright, citrus note in warming dishes like Hot Pot with Black Cod and Mushrooms (page 96). Traditionally made with Japanese citrus, lemon and orange juices help approximate the flavor in this recipe.

½ cup fresh lemon juice (about 4 lemons)

¼ cup fresh navel orange juice (about 1 large orange)

Scant ¾ cup soy sauce or tamari

1 (7-inch) piece kombu, cut to fit if needed

1 cup loosely packed bonito flakes

1. Combine the lemon juice, orange juice, soy sauce, kombu, and bonito flakes in a mason jar or other container with a tight-fitting lid.

2. Let steep in the refrigerator for at least 2 days; the flavors will further develop for up to 2 weeks.

3. When ready to use, strain the mixture into another jar. Remove and discard the kombu. Squeeze the liquid out of the bonito flakes, then discard them. Cover the ponzu and store in the refrigerator for up to 6 months.

INGREDIENT TIP: Ponzu can be used to make a quick dressing or marinade: Whisk together 2 tablespoons ponzu, 1 teaspoon sugar, and 1 teaspoon toasted sesame oil.

Sushizu

SUSHI VINEGAR

Gluten-Free, Nut-Free, One Pot, 30 Minutes or Less, Vegan

PREP TIME: 5 MINUTES | MAKES ABOUT 1¼ CUPS

Sushi vinegar is often sold in the Asian or international section at the grocery store as "seasoned rice vinegar." It's incredibly easy to make at home, so there's no need to buy the bottled stuff. Having this mixture ready in the refrigerator makes it convenient to make Sushi Bowls (page 103), Mixed-Vegetable Sushi Rice (page 78), and DIY Hand Roll Sushi (page 104), even on a weeknight. I recommend using 6 tablespoons for every recipe of Basic Short-Grain Rice (page 16).

---

1 cup rice vinegar

6 tablespoons sugar

2 tablespoons salt

1. Combine the vinegar, sugar, and salt in a mason jar or other container with a tight-fitting lid.

2. Shake until the sugar and salt have dissolved. Store in the refrigerator for up to a year.

Kaeshi

SWEET SOY CONCENTRATE

Gluten-Free, Nut-Free, One Pot, 30 Minutes or Less, Vegan

PREP TIME: 5 MINUTES | COOK TIME: 10 MINUTES | MAKES ABOUT 1¼ CUPS

Kaeshi is a concentrated sauce that's convenient to have ready to go in your refrigerator because it can make a meal in an instant. When making noodle soups and dipping sauces, all you need to do is add the required amount of dashi. My teenage stepdaughter often makes scrambled eggs and rice for breakfast or a snack, and this is a ready-made seasoning that she can easily add.

¼ cup mirin

⅓ cup sugar

1 cup soy sauce or tamari

1. Put the mirin in a small pot and cook over medium heat for 5 minutes.

2. Add the sugar and whisk until it has dissolved.

3. Add the soy sauce and cook for another 5 minutes.

4. Transfer to a mason jar or container with a tight-fitting lid to cool.

5. Cover and store in the refrigerator for up to 3 months.

TONKATSU SAUCE

Gluten-Free, Nut-Free, One Pot, 30 Minutes or Less

PREP TIME: 5 MINUTES | MAKES ½ CUP

The Bull Dog brand of tonkatsu sauce comes in a rounded rectangular bottle with a retro label design and has a particular way you snap the top on and off. The fact that it was an iconic Japanese condiment and an unquestioned fixture in our refrigerator door made me never wonder how to make it myself. But once I tried, I realized how simple it was. It's savory and slightly sweet and used to accompany fried foods like Mashed Potato Bake (page 64) and Panko Fried Shrimp (page 100).

---

3 tablespoons
   Worcestershire sauce

2 tablespoons ketchup

1 tablespoon soy sauce
   or tamari

1 tablespoon mayonnaise

1 tablespoon tahini

1 teaspoon sugar

1. In a medium bowl, whisk together the Worcestershire sauce, ketchup, soy sauce, mayonnaise, tahini, and sugar until the sugar has dissolved.

2. Store in a mason jar or other container with a tight-fitting lid in the refrigerator for up to 3 months.

CHAPTER THREE

SNACKS AND SALADS

COCONUT, ALMOND, AND MATCHA GRANOLA

Gluten-Free, Vegetarian

PREP TIME: 10 MINUTES | COOK TIME: 40 MINUTES | MAKES ABOUT 4 CUPS

Matcha, a bright green tea powder made from shade-grown tea leaves, has recently gained popularity in the United States. There are three grades: ceremonial, premium (or universal), and culinary. For this recipe you'll want premium or culinary. Here, matcha gives the granola a mild, almost grassy flavor that complements the sweetness of the other ingredients. Eat this as a cereal with milk, use it as a topping for yogurt, or munch on it with a cup of tea as a snack. I advise against using white chocolate chips since an additive prevents proper melting.

2½ cups crispy brown rice cereal

1¾ cups gluten-free rolled oats

¼ cup unsweetened coconut flakes

¼ cup sliced almonds

1½ tablespoons matcha

½ teaspoon salt

¼ cup coconut oil

1½ ounces white chocolate (about a third of a 4.4-ounce bar), coarsely chopped

¼ cup brown rice syrup

1. Preheat the oven to 275°F. Line a rimmed baking sheet with parchment paper.

2. In a large bowl, toss together the rice cereal, oats, coconut flakes, almonds, matcha, and salt. Set aside.

3. Pour an inch of water into a small pot. Bring the water to a boil over medium-high heat, then turn the heat to low. Place a metal bowl big enough to sit in the pot (but not touch the water) on top. Combine the coconut oil and white chocolate in the bowl and stir until melted, about 1 minute.

4. Turn off the heat and remove the bowl from the pot. Whisk the brown rice syrup into the chocolate mixture until well combined.

5. Pour the chocolate mixture over the oat mixture and use a silicone spatula to carefully mix with broad strokes. Continue to mix until it is evenly coated (no dry bits, no clumps of syrup). Pour the mixture onto the lined baking sheet and spread it out in an even layer.

6. Bake until the granola has lightly browned, about 35 minutes. Remove from the oven and give it a toss while it is still hot, then set aside to cool completely. Store in an airtight container at room temperature for up to 2 weeks.

FURIKAKE POPCORN

Gluten-Free, Nut-Free, One Pot, 30 Minutes or Less, Vegan

PREP TIME: 5 MINUTES **|** COOK TIME: 5 MINUTES **|** SERVES 2 TO 3

This was part of our nighttime habit for a while. My husband and I would pop on Netflix and watch *Terrace House* (for you TeraHa fans, an omuraisu recipe is on page 70) after our daughter went to bed. The furikake has savory notes from the seaweed and gets that addictive salty-sweet balance just right. I have a hard time going back to straight buttered popcorn after this. Two tablespoons of furikake may seem like a lot, but keep in mind some of it will end up at the bottom of the bowl.

---

2 tablespoons coconut oil

⅓ cup popcorn kernels

3 teaspoons olive oil, divided

2 tablespoons aji nori furikake

1. In a medium pot, heat the coconut oil over medium-low to medium heat for 2 minutes. Add the popcorn kernels and cover.

2. Sit tight as the popcorn pops. After 1½ to 2 minutes, you should hear 5 seconds of silence between pops; at this point, immediately turn off the heat and empty the popcorn into a large bowl.

3. Lightly drizzle the popcorn with 1 teaspoon olive oil and sprinkle some furikake on top. The oil will help the furikake stick to the popcorn. Toss to combine and repeat two more times until the popcorn is coated with furikake.

INGREDIENT TIP: If you have a spray olive oil, use it to get a more even coating.

YOKO'S SESAME DIP

Gluten-Free, Nut-Free, 30 Minutes or Less, Vegetarian

PREP TIME: 10 MINUTES | MAKES ABOUT ½ CUP

I get my love of cooking and eating from my mom. She made it look easy and effortless, which is probably because she found joy in the process. Everything she made when I was growing up was delicious, and because of that I was the kid who ate practically anything. This dip is one of her recipes. While optional, I recommend adding the wasabi since it imparts a nice flavor and kick. Start with a small amount and work your way up to 2 teaspoons if you're sensitive to heat. This dip goes great with steamed broccoli, green beans, snap peas, sliced cucumbers, cherry tomatoes, or any other crudité.

2 tablespoons toasted sesame seeds

¼ cup mayonnaise

2 teaspoons sugar

2 teaspoons rice vinegar

2 teaspoons wasabi (optional)

1. Put the sesame seeds in a coffee or spice grinder and quickly pulse 8 times.

2. Empty the seeds into a medium bowl. Add the mayonnaise, sugar, vinegar, and wasabi (if using), and mix until well combined.

EASY CUCUMBER PICKLES

Gluten-Free, Nut-Free, One Pot, Vegan

PREP TIME: 15 MINUTES | MARINATE TIME: 8 HOURS | SERVES 4

Pickles are an essential part of a Japanese meal. There are many pickling methods and ingredients, all worthy of a book in and of itself. During each meal, usually only a few pieces are needed to nibble on and eat with rice. They should act as an accent and occasionally punctuate the meal. The longer the cucumbers marinate in the dressing, the saltier they will be. For this recipe, the cucumbers should sit overnight, though you could also eat them right away for a tangy cucumber salad.

---

1 tablespoon sugar

1 tablespoon soy sauce
or tamari

1 tablespoon rice vinegar

1 tablespoon water

1 small garlic
clove, minced

1 scallion, white and
green parts, chopped

2 Persian cucumbers, cut
into 1-inch pieces

1. In a medium bowl, whisk together the sugar, soy sauce, vinegar, water, garlic, and scallion until the sugar has dissolved.

2. Add the cucumbers and toss to coat with the dressing. Cover and let marinate overnight before serving.

PREP TIP: A batch of these cucumbers, Salted Salmon (page 92), Miso Soup (page 20), and rice make for an easy breakfast. The night before, I usually wash and soak the rice, and cut the vegetables and set a pot of water with kombu for the miso soup. The next morning, I cook the rice, make the dashi and miso soup, and bake the salmon. It may sound like a lot of work, but it is mostly hands-off. Sometimes I'll make a quick list of tasks the night before so I can be efficient, even when I'm half awake.

MISO-MARINATED EGGS

Gluten-Free, Nut-Free, Vegetarian

PREP TIME: 10 MINUTES | COOK TIME: 10 MINUTES | MARINATE TIME: 8 HOURS | MAKES 6 EGGS

I like my eggs to have a jammy yolk, and after much trial and error, this method gave me the most consistent results. Taking the eggs straight from the refrigerator and adding them to the boiling water makes the starting temperature of all the elements predictable. After a relatively short boil, I scoop the eggs out and let them cool on the counter so the yolks continue to gently cook in their shells. If you like your egg yolks cooked hard, boil them for a couple minutes more.

---

6 large eggs, refrigerated

2 tablespoons mirin

1½ tablespoons sake

¼ cup miso

1. Fill a medium pot with enough water to cover the eggs. Cover the pot and bring the water to a boil over medium heat. Once boiling, take the eggs out of the refrigerator and carefully ease them into the water with a ladle or spoon. Boil, uncovered, for 6 minutes.

2. Remove the eggs from the water with a slotted spoon and set them on a plate to cool for 1 hour.

3. Meanwhile, in a small pot, combine the mirin and sake and bring to a boil over medium heat. Turn the heat to low and simmer for 2 minutes. Remove from the heat and let sit for 5 minutes. Whisk in the miso.

4. Peel the eggs and place them in a zip-top plastic bag. Add the miso mixture and gently move the eggs around to evenly coat them with the marinade. Seal the bag, making sure to squeeze out as much air as possible.

5. Marinate the eggs in the refrigerator at least overnight, or for up to 1 week.

6. To serve, rinse off the miso mixture and slice in half.

ON BALANCE

Balance is an important consideration in Japanese aesthetics. This includes cooking, too. When it comes to food, different elements are taken into account, including flavor, texture, type of ingredient, and color.

For example, if a dish is heavily seasoned and rich, like Ginger Pork with Green Cabbage and Rice (page 111), it is counterbalanced with something fresh and light, like thinly sliced cabbage. If a dish has a soft and smooth texture, like Japanese Potato Salad (page 43), it can be paired with something crunchy or crisp, like Sweet Stir-Fried Carrots and Burdock Root (page 61). Something savory and slightly sweet, like Classic Teriyaki Chicken (page 109), can be paired with something salty or sour, like Green Salad with Sesame-Miso Dressing (page 38).

The meal should also consider visual contrast by coordinating a variety of colors and shapes. If you ever look through a Japanese bento cookbook, you'll notice there is often a section that features recipes according to color. This is so you can easily find a recipe if you're missing a certain color to balance the overall aesthetic of your dish. These visual considerations make a meal appetizing to the eyes well before you take the first bite.

GREEN SALAD WITH SESAME-MISO DRESSING

Gluten-Free, Nut-Free, 30 Minutes or Less, Vegetarian

PREP TIME: 15 MINUTES | SERVES 4

Having some kind of small salad at each meal is typical in Japanese cuisine. This sesame-miso dressing is on the thick side and clings nicely to the shredded vegetables. It's creamy from the tahini, salty and rich from the miso, acidic from the vinegar, and lightly sweet from the honey. When I make salad dressings, especially this one, I usually double the batch and store the remainder in the refrigerator to use throughout the week.

2 tablespoons rice vinegar

2 tablespoons tahini

1 tablespoon miso

1½ teaspoons honey

1 teaspoon water

2 cups shredded romaine lettuce

1 cup thinly sliced green cabbage

1 (3-inch) section English cucumber, julienned

4 shiso leaves, thinly sliced (optional)

1. In a small bowl, whisk together the vinegar, tahini, miso, honey, and water.

2. In a large bowl, toss together the lettuce, cabbage, cucumber, and shiso (if using).

3. Portion out the salad onto 4 plates and spoon the dressing over it. Serve immediately.

TOMATO AND SHISO SALAD

Gluten-Free, Nut-Free, 30 Minutes or Less, Vegan

PREP TIME: 15 MINUTES **|** SERVES 4

Just as tomatoes and basil are thought to have a natural affinity, so do tomatoes and shiso. My mom, with her incredible green thumb, had a vegetable garden where both would proliferate in the summer. We have an amazing variety of tomatoes in California, and I would recommend getting the most flavorful ones you can find when you make this salad at home.

1 small onion, minced

1 tablespoon soy sauce
  or tamari

2 teaspoons toasted
  sesame oil

1 teaspoon rice vinegar

Pinch ground
  white pepper

2 tomatoes, sliced

6 shiso leaves, minced

1. Put the minced onion in a small bowl and cover with water. Let soak for 5 minutes, then drain and pat dry.

2. In another small bowl, whisk together the soy sauce, sesame oil, vinegar, and white pepper.

3. Arrange the tomatoes on a plate, top with the onion, and then add the shiso. Drizzle the dressing over top and serve.

PREP TIP: Soaking the raw onion in water will help lessen some of the sharpness. Soak for longer if the onion is particularly strong.

VARIATION TIP: If you can't find shiso, an equal mix of mint and basil is a good substitute.

POTLUCK-READY CRUNCHY CABBAGE SALAD

Gluten-Free, 30 Minutes or Less, Vegetarian

PREP TIME: 25 MINUTES | COOK TIME: 5 MINUTES | SERVES 15 TO 20

At potlucks, rarely is a salad something to *ooh* and *ahh* over, but this salad never disappoints. In fact, I receive compliments and recipe requests every time, without fail. The combination of fresh cabbage and toasted almonds provides plenty of crunch, and the fact that it's a hearty salad that can sit and hold its integrity is a plus. On top of all that, it's fast and easy to prepare, making it my all-time favorite potluck dish.

---

1 medium cabbage

4 tablespoons (½ stick) unsalted butter

2 cups roasted almonds, chopped

⅓ cup toasted sesame seeds

½ cup olive oil

¼ cup sugar

2 tablespoons rice vinegar

2 tablespoons soy sauce or tamari

5 scallions, white and green parts, chopped

1. Core the cabbage and run it through a food processor fitted with the slicing disk. Alternatively, you can thinly slice the cabbage by hand. Set aside.

2. In a large skillet, melt the butter over medium heat. Add the almonds, stir to coat with the butter, and allow them to warm for a couple minutes. Add the sesame seeds and stir to combine, being careful not to let them burn. Once warm and smelling fragrant, 1 or 2 minutes, scrape onto a plate to completely cool.

3. In a small jar, combine the olive oil, sugar, vinegar, and soy sauce. Cover and shake until the sugar has dissolved.

4. In a large salad bowl, toss the cabbage, scallions, and almond mixture. Pour the dressing over the top, toss thoroughly, and serve.

INGREDIENT TIP: I buy roasted almonds and toasted sesame seeds because I find it difficult to toast both of them evenly on the stove.

TOFU SALAD WITH SESAME DRESSING

Gluten-Free, Nut-Free, 30 Minutes or Less, Vegan

PREP TIME: 20 MINUTES | SERVES 4

This is not a salad with a little tofu. This is a block of tofu with a bunch of vegetables, drizzled with a sesame dressing. It's a hearty salad, but not one that will leave you feeling heavy. It's particularly good in the summer months, when the heat might slow your appetite but you still want something satisfying.

---

1 (14-ounce) package soft tofu

½ onion, sliced

3 small pinches dried wakame

1 garlic clove, grated

1 (½-inch) piece ginger, peeled and grated

1 tablespoon minced scallion

4 teaspoons soy sauce or tamari

4 teaspoons rice vinegar

1 tablespoon toasted sesame oil

1 teaspoon sugar

2 tomatoes, halved, cored, and sliced

1 (6-inch) section English cucumber, sliced on a diagonal and julienned

1. Drain the tofu and wrap it in a paper towel; place it on a plate and set aside.

2. Put the sliced onion in a small bowl, cover with water, and set aside.

3. Put the dried wakame in another small bowl, cover with water, and set aside.

4. In a small jar, combine the garlic, ginger, scallion, soy sauce, vinegar, sesame oil, and sugar. Cover and shake to combine.

5. Unwrap the tofu, cut it in half lengthwise, then cut it crosswise into ½-inch slices. Line the tofu slices, slightly overlapping, down the center of a plate. Arrange the tomato and cucumber around the tofu.

6. Drain the onion and pat dry. Top the tofu with the onion. Squeeze the wakame to remove any excess water, then place bits of it over the whole salad.

7. Spoon the desired amount of dressing over top. Store any extra dressing in the refrigerator for up to a few days.

SWEET AND TANGY TUNA AND CARROT SALAD

Gluten-Free, Nut-Free, 30 Minutes or Less

PREP TIME: 20 MINUTES | COOK TIME: 10 MINUTES, PLUS 1 HOUR TO CHILL | SERVES 4

Something about this combination of flavors—the Dijon mustard and the soy sauce—allows this salad go well with either a Japanese or Western meal. The ingredients are easy to find and it keeps well, making it good for packing in a lunch the next day. If you can find shiso, I recommend using it because it gives the salad a herbaceous boost.

1 tablespoon
  Dijon mustard

1 tablespoon rice vinegar

1 tablespoon fresh
  lemon juice

¼ teaspoon soy sauce
  or tamari

Pinch freshly ground
  black pepper

1 tablespoon avocado oil

2 small shallots,
  finely chopped

1 large garlic
  clove, minced

4 medium carrots, thinly
  sliced on a diagonal and
  julienned

1 (5-ounce) can solid
  white tuna, drained

2 shiso leaves, thinly
  sliced (optional)

1. In a small bowl, whisk together the mustard, vinegar, lemon juice, soy sauce, and pepper. Set aside.

2. In a large skillet, heat the oil over medium heat. Add the shallots and cook, stirring occasionally, until translucent, 2 to 3 minutes. Add the garlic and cook until fragrant, about 30 seconds.

3. Add the carrots and cook, stirring constantly, until they are softened but not mushy, about 5 minutes. Transfer the vegetables to a large bowl.

4. Add the tuna and the dressing to the bowl and mix until thoroughly combined, breaking up the tuna with a wooden spoon. Cool to room temperature or in the refrigerator for about 1 hour to let the flavors meld.

5. Top with the shiso (if using) and serve.

JAPANESE POTATO SALAD

Gluten-Free, Nut-Free

PREP TIME: 25 MINUTES | COOK TIME: 15 MINUTES, PLUS 1 HOUR TO CHILL | SERVES 4

There may be strong opinions about Japanese potato salad and Kewpie mayonnaise. If you've never seen the Japanese brand of mayonnaise, it comes in a squeeze bottle, sort of in the shape of a pastry bag, with a red cap. It has a star-shaped tip and its logo is a kewpie doll. Pretty iconic. The flavor is richer and creamier than American mayonnaise, and I will make the (possibly) controversial claim that I prefer Best Foods. It's what I grew up on and what inevitably tastes "right" to me when it comes to mayonnaise. All this is to say: Use what tastes right to you!

---

2 large russet potatoes, peeled and cut into 1-inch pieces

1 (3-inch) segment English cucumber, quartered lengthwise and thinly sliced crosswise

¼ cup thinly sliced onion

¾ teaspoon salt, divided

1 tablespoon rice vinegar

2 slices ham, thinly sliced into 1-inch strips

¼ cup mayonnaise

Pinch ground white pepper

1. Pour an inch of water into a large pot. Cover and bring to a boil over medium-high heat. Put the potatoes in a metal steamer basket and place the basket in the pot. Cover, turn the heat to medium-low, and steam the potatoes until soft, about 15 minutes.

2. While the potatoes are cooking, combine the cucumber and onion in a small bowl and sprinkle with ¼ teaspoon salt. Massage the vegetables with your fingers until the salt is incorporated and let them sit until the moisture is drawn out, about 15 minutes.

3. When the potatoes are done, empty them into a large bowl, and add the vinegar and remaining ½ teaspoon salt. Mix to combine. Mash the potatoes so you have some large pieces and some small, bite-size bits.

4. Squeeze as much moisture as you can from the cucumber and onion, one handful at a time, and add to the bowl with the potatoes.

5. Add the ham, mayonnaise, and pepper and mix well to combine. Let cool, then refrigerate for at least 1 hour before serving.

Onigiri, Omusubi

BONITO RICE BALLS

Gluten-Free, Nut-Free

PREP TIME: 15 MINUTES **|** MAKES 8 RICE BALLS

Although they're called "balls," these perfect portable snacks are usually triangular in shape. They're also endlessly customizable: You can mix an ingredient into the rice to season it, or create a little hole in the center and fill it with some leftover Japanese "Fried" Chicken (page 118) or Panko Fried Shrimp (page 100). It might take a little practice to get used to shaping them, but once you get the hang of it, it takes no time at all. I recommend looking up a how-to video first, as it is helpful to see how this comes together, or take a look at my tip on the next page for a shortcut.

2 tablespoons salt

1 recipe Basic Short-Grain Rice (page 16)

¼ cup Bonito Rice Topping (page 24)

2 sheets Japanese sushi nori, quartered lengthwise and halved crosswise

1. Set out a small bowl of water and put the salt on a small plate.

2. Put the rice in a large bowl. Add the bonito rice topping and use a wet rice paddle or silicone spatula to mix it into the rice by alternately using a slicing motion and scooping and flipping the rice from the bottom to the top to incorporate it. Be careful not to crush the grains of rice.

3. Wet your rice paddle or spatula again and use it to divide the rice into 8 even portions.

4. Generously wet both hands in the bowl of water, dip two fingers in the salt, and smear it in the palm of your other hand. Dip and smear again and then rub your hands together a couple of times so the salt dissolves a little and evenly distributes onto your palms. There will be salt left at the end of the process.

5. Scoop one portion of rice into your nondominant hand. To shape the rice ball, imagine a triangle and angle your dominant hand in the shape of the peak of the triangle. Press down on the rice while your other hand is wrapped around the bottom of the rice ball. The bottom part of your palm and your fingers on your nondominant hand should press on either side of the flat sides.

6. Press the rice together, then rotate it so one of the bottom corners of the triangle is at the top and press again. Repeat this motion until the rice holds together.

7. Wrap the rice ball with one piece of nori. Repeat with the remaining portions of rice.

PREP TIP: If the triangular shape is difficult to master, you can place the portioned rice on a piece of plastic wrap. Gather up the wrap around the rice and twist so that you have a small ball of rice, then press together so it will hold its shape.

VEGETARIAN DISHES

Hōrensō No Shiraae

SPINACH DRESSED WITH TOFU

Gluten-Free, Nut-Free, 30 Minutes or Less, Vegan

PREP TIME: 20 MINUTES | COOK TIME: 5 MINUTES | SERVES 4

This dish has the gentle flavor of sesame, the richness of miso, the creaminess of tofu, and soft steamed spinach to create a delicate combination. It's low in oil and could serve as the protein base alongside a number of the meatless recipes in this book. For example, try serving it with Football Sushi (page 76), Mushrooms with Butter Ponzu (page 55), and Miso Soup (page 20).

½ (14-ounce) package soft tofu

1 medium bunch spinach (not baby spinach), trimmed

2 tablespoons tahini

1 tablespoon sugar

2 teaspoons soy sauce or tamari

1 teaspoon miso (see Ingredient Tip)

1. Wrap the tofu in a paper towel. Place on a plate and put another plate on top. Let it sit for at least 15 minutes to press out some of the water.

2. Meanwhile, pour an inch of water into a large pot. Cover and bring to a boil over medium-high heat. Put the spinach in a metal steamer basket and place the basket in the pot. Cover, turn the heat to medium-low, and steam the spinach for 3 minutes.

3. Use a pair of tongs to transfer the spinach to a fine-mesh strainer to cool. When cool enough to touch, squeeze the water out of the spinach, a handful at a time. Roughly chop and set aside.

4. In a medium bowl, combine the tahini, sugar, soy sauce, and miso. Roughly crumble the tofu into the bowl with your hands.

5. With a fork, mash and combine the ingredients until you have a semi-smooth paste. Add the spinach and mix well until combined. Serve.

> **INGREDIENT TIP:** The saltiness of miso varies, so start with 1 teaspoon and taste to see if it needs more. The flavors should be well balanced and not too sweet or salty.

Hōrensō No Kurumi Ae

SPINACH DRESSED WITH WALNUTS

Gluten-Free, 30 Minutes or Less, Vegan

PREP TIME: 15 MINUTES | COOK TIME: 5 MINUTES | SERVES 4

Have you ever tried walnut butter? It's glorious. A few years ago, I discovered how easy it is to make nut butters at home. Roasted walnuts have an amazingly robust flavor and are touted for being high in omega-3s and antioxidants. For this recipe, be sure to use fresh walnuts because they go rancid quickly and develop an unappealing bitter taste.

---

1 large bunch spinach (not baby spinach), trimmed

½ cup walnuts, toasted and cooled

1 tablespoon soy sauce or tamari

1½ teaspoons sugar

1 teaspoon mirin

1. Pour an inch of water into a large pot. Cover and bring to a boil over medium-high heat. Put the spinach in a metal steamer basket and place the basket in the pot. Cover, turn the heat to medium-low, and steam the spinach for 3 minutes.

2. Use a pair of tongs to transfer the spinach to a fine-mesh strainer to cool. When cool enough to touch, squeeze the water out of the spinach, a handful at a time. Roughly chop and set aside.

3. Put the walnuts in a food processor and run until the walnuts are mostly ground but some little bits remain. The walnuts shouldn't be fully ground into a paste.

4. In a medium bowl, whisk together the soy sauce, sugar, and mirin. Whisk in the walnuts. Add the spinach and mix with chopsticks until thoroughly combined. Serve.

Hiyayakko

COLD TOFU, THREE WAYS

Gluten-Free, Nut-Free, 30 Minutes or Less

PREP TIME: 10 MINUTES | EACH WAY SERVES 4

My dad always emphasized the importance of protein when I was growing up. As far as I can remember, tofu was almost always served at dinner. Cold tofu is one of the easiest side dishes to make because there's no cooking involved. If you can find artisanal tofu where you live, this is where it can really shine. For a complete vegetarian meal, serve any of these cold tofu dishes with Sweet Stir-Fried Carrots and Burdock Root (page 61), Garlicky Shoyu Poblanos (page 59), Miso Soup (page 20), and rice.

FIRST WAY

½ (14-ounce) package soft tofu, quartered

1 (½-inch) piece ginger, peeled and grated

½ scallion, white and green parts, chopped

4 tablespoons Dashi Soy Sauce (page 25), divided

1. Place the 4 pieces of tofu on small plates.

2. Divide the ginger and scallion evenly over each piece of tofu.

3. Drizzle each piece with 1 tablespoon dashi soy sauce. Serve.

SECOND WAY

½ (14-ounce) package soft tofu, quartered

2 shiso leaves, minced

½ avocado, mashed

4 tablespoons Citrus Soy Sauce (page 26), divided

1. Place the 4 pieces of tofu on small plates.

2. Mix the shiso and avocado in a small bowl until combined.

3. Divide the shiso-avocado mixture evenly over each piece of tofu.

4. Drizzle each with 1 tablespoon citrus soy sauce. Serve.

THIRD WAY

½ (14-ounce) package soft tofu, quartered

Pinch bonito flakes

1 teaspoon sesame seeds, divided

4 tablespoons Sweet Soy Concentrate (page 28), divided

1. Place the 4 pieces of tofu on small plates.

2. Rub the bonito flakes with your fingers in a small bowl to break up the flakes. Divide them evenly over each piece of tofu.

3. Sprinkle ¼ teaspoon sesame seeds on each piece.

4. Drizzle each with 1 tablespoon sweet soy concentrate. Serve.

Sayaingen No Goma Ae

GREEN BEANS WITH SESAME

Gluten-Free, Nut-Free, 30 Minutes or Less, Vegan

PREP TIME: 10 MINUTES | COOK TIME: 10 MINUTES | SERVES 6

This classic Japanese recipe is one of those side dishes you often see tucked into a corner of a bento. It's so simple that it's easily overlooked, but it has always been one of my favorites. If green beans are not in season, you can use broccoli, asparagus, or sugar snap peas. Another variation is to use black sesame seeds, which add a deeper flavor and more dramatic look.

---

8 ounces green
   beans, trimmed

3 tablespoons toasted
   sesame seeds

1 tablespoon soy sauce
   or tamari

1 tablespoon mirin

1. Pour an inch of water into a large pot. Cover and bring to a boil over medium-high heat. Put the green beans in a metal steamer basket and place the basket in the pot. Cover the pot, turn the heat to medium-low, and steam the green beans until soft, about 6 minutes, depending on the thickness of the beans. Transfer the green beans to a plate to cool slightly.

2. Put the sesame seeds in a coffee or spice grinder and quickly pulse 6 times. Be careful not to overgrind; you still want some whole seeds.

3. Empty the seeds into a medium bowl. Add the soy sauce and mirin and stir to combine.

4. When the green beans are cool enough to handle, cut them into 1½-inch pieces. While still warm, add the green beans to the bowl with the sesame seed mixture and toss to combine. Serve warm or at room temperature.

PREP TIP: Before using a coffee grinder for the sesame seeds, use a pastry brush (not silicone) to remove any small grounds of coffee in the grinder. Add a tablespoon of uncooked rice and pulse until ground into a fine powder. Empty the contents and use the brush again to get rid of any powdery remnants. This should help remove any residual coffee grounds.

STIR-FRIED BROCCOLI WITH CRISPY GARLIC

Gluten-Free, Nut-Free, One Pot, 30 Minutes or Less

PREP TIME: 10 MINUTES | COOK TIME: 15 MINUTES | SERVES 3

Like many parents, I am often encouraging my daughter to eat more vegetables. One day she'll happily eat daikon and the next time it comes around she'll say she doesn't like it. But consistently, she is okay with broccoli. Broccoli often becomes the default vegetable because she is completely content eating it steamed and plain. While steamed broccoli *is* delicious, sometimes the adults want a little more flavor.

---

2 small heads broccoli

1 tablespoon avocado oil

2 garlic cloves, thinly sliced

2 tablespoons water

1 teaspoon soy sauce or tamari

Pinch bonito flakes

1. Cut the broccoli into small florets. Peel the outer skin of the stem and slice crosswise into 1-inch pieces.

2. In a medium skillet, heat the oil over medium heat and fry the garlic until golden and crispy, about 2 minutes. Remove the garlic slices with a slotted spoon and set aside.

3. Add the broccoli to the pan and toss to coat with oil. Add the water, cover, and turn the heat to low. Let it cook for 4 minutes.

4. Uncover and turn the heat back up to medium. Toss the broccoli pieces and shake the pan so that there's an even layer of broccoli. Let it cook undisturbed for 1 minute. Toss the pieces again and shake. Let it cook undisturbed for 1 more minute.

5. Turn the heat to low, return the garlic to the pan, and toss again. Add the soy sauce, toss to combine, and cook off any excess liquid.

6. Rub the bonito flakes with your fingers as you sprinkle them over the broccoli. Serve.

PREP TIP: Caramelization adds a lot of flavor, so it's important to leave the broccoli alone for a minute to get a nice char. When browning the garlic, keep an eye on it because it burns quickly.

Satsumaimo No Lemon Ni

JAPANESE SWEET POTATO WITH LEMON

Gluten-Free, Nut-Free, Vegetarian

PREP TIME: 15 MINUTES, PLUS 10 MINUTES TO SOAK

COOK TIME: 10 MINUTES | CHILL TIME: 3 HOURS | SERVES 4

Most mornings, I'm hurriedly making breakfast and lunch and packing a snack. This dish requires a rest in the refrigerator and should be eaten cold, so the fact that I can take it directly from the refrigerator and pack it in a bento box for lunch is a win. Serve it in combination with salty dishes, such as Pan-Tossed Garlicky Green Beans and Pork (page 110) or Ginger Pork with Green Cabbage and Rice (page 111), as it is nice to have something sweet and perky to awaken the palate.

---

1 medium Japanese sweet potato, scrubbed and cut crosswise into ½-inch slices

2 tablespoons honey

3 thin lemon slices

1. Soak the sweet potato slices in a bowl of water for 10 minutes, then drain. Put them in a medium pot and pour in water until they are barely covered.

2. Spoon the honey into the pot and top with the lemon slices. Bring to a boil over medium heat, then turn the heat down to medium-low and cook until the sweet potatoes are soft but not falling apart, about 10 minutes.

3. Let cool, then cover and refrigerate for at least 3 hours before serving.

VARIATION TIP: Use 2½ tablespoons sugar instead of the honey to make this dish vegan.

Kofuki Imo

BUTTERY SWEET POTATOES

Gluten-Free, Nut-Free, 30 Minutes or Less, Vegetarian

PREP TIME: 10 MINUTES | COOK TIME: 20 MINUTES | SERVES 4

These potatoes are, quite honestly, like candy. This dish is not meant to be a main component of a meal, but a small side to enjoy with other dishes. Pair it with Stir-Fried Broccoli with Crispy Garlic (page 52) and a protein of your choice.

---

3 small Japanese sweet potatoes, peeled and cut crosswise into 1¼-inch pieces

1 heaping tablespoon soy sauce or tamari

1½ teaspoons mirin

1 tablespoon unsalted butter

1. Pour an inch of water into a large pot. Cover and bring to a boil over medium-high heat. Put the potatoes in a metal steamer basket and place the basket in the pot. Cover the pot, turn the heat to medium-low, and steam the potatoes until soft, about 15 minutes.

2. Transfer the potatoes to a plate to cool slightly, then cut them into thick half-moon pieces.

3. Combine the soy sauce and mirin in a medium skillet and heat over medium heat. When small bubbles begin to appear, add the potatoes and toss to coat. Cook until all the liquid is gone, about 1 minute. Turn off the heat and add the butter. Stir until the butter is melted and the potatoes are coated evenly. Serve warm.

VARIATION TIP: You can substitute a white sweet potato (but not the orange-fleshed variety) for the Japanese sweet potato. Add more mirin, if you do.

MUSHROOMS WITH BUTTER PONZU

Gluten-Free, Nut-Free, 30 Minutes or Less

PREP TIME: 5 MINUTES | COOK TIME: 15 MINUTES | SERVES 4

This is a dish for mushroom lovers. The tart ponzu mellows and sweetens nicely with the addition of the butter. Feel free to substitute oyster mushrooms if beech mushrooms are hard to find, or use a variety. If you've made the ponzu ahead of time, this dish packs in a lot of flavor in no time at all. Serve with Salted Salmon (page 92) and Sweet Soy-Braised Eggplant (page 58).

---

1 tablespoon unsalted butter, divided

2 (3.5-ounce) packages beech mushrooms, trimmed and separated by hand

3 tablespoons Citrus Soy Sauce (page 26)

2 tablespoons chopped chives, for garnish

1. Melt ½ tablespoon (1½ teaspoons) butter in a medium pan over medium heat. Add the mushrooms and toss to coat. The mushrooms will look dry at first, but they will start to release their moisture after about 5 minutes.

2. Continue cooking, stirring occasionally, until the mushrooms soften and have browned in some areas, about 5 minutes more.

3. Add the citrus soy sauce and cook until most of the moisture has evaporated, about 3 minutes.

4. Turn off the heat and add the remaining ½ tablespoon (1½ teaspoons) butter and stir until melted. Serve the mushrooms topped with the chives.

SIMMERED KABOCHA

Gluten-Free, Nut-Free

PREP TIME: 20 MINUTES **|** COOK TIME: 20 MINUTES **|** SERVES 4

My father's mother, who helped raise me, was the quintessential grandmother. She was kind and wise, possessed immense internal strength, and was an amazing cook. She would watch cooking shows while I was at school and cooked a wide variety of things for us. Kabocha reminds me of her because she cooked it frequently in the colder months, telling me it had cancer-preventing benefits. The flavors in this dish will meld nicely over a few days, and it is delicious eaten cold.

½ medium kabocha, seeded and cut into 1½-inch pieces

2 tablespoons avocado oil

1 cup Basic Dashi (page 18) or Vegan Dashi (page 19)

1 tablespoon sugar

1 tablespoon mirin

1 tablespoon soy sauce or tamari

1. With a vegetable peeler, swipe the edge off the corners of each piece of kabocha, where the skin meets the flesh on all 4 sides (see page 57).

2. Heat the oil in a large pot over medium heat. Add the kabocha and stir, coating the pieces evenly with oil. When the kabocha flesh turns bright orange, about 2 minutes, add the dashi. Bring to a boil, then carefully spoon off any foam that rises to the surface.

3. Stir in the sugar and mirin and cook for 4 to 5 minutes, stirring occasionally.

4. Add the soy sauce and lower the heat to a simmer. If there isn't much liquid to cover the kabocha, cut a piece of aluminum foil to fit inside your pot. Press the foil down into the pot so it sits on the surface of the kabocha. Cook for another 10 minutes, stirring and swirling the dashi mixture to coat the kabocha occasionally. Taste the dashi and add more soy sauce if it's too sweet or more mirin if it's too salty.

5. Insert a toothpick into a piece of kabocha—if it slides in easily, it's done. Serve

VARIATION TIP: Butternut squash can be used in place of the kabocha. Reduce the amount of sugar if making this substitution.

HOW TO SAFELY PREP KABOCHA

When cutting into kabocha squash, the first cut can be dangerous, so it's extremely important to use a sharp knife.

1. Hold the kabocha steady and insert the tip of your knife into the top, next to the stem.

2. Press down firmly until the knife goes through to the bottom, cutting through half of the kabocha.

3. Carefully remove the knife and turn the kabocha over, then insert the knife in the slit you just made to finish cutting it all the way through.

The edges of the kabocha pieces, where the skin meets the flesh, will be very sharp. In the recipe on the previous page, I suggest running a vegetable peeler along this edge to help the kabocha stay intact and be more visually appealing. When simmering, the edges will nudge each other and cause the kabocha to break down. If this is too laborious, feel free to skip the first step.

Nasu No Itameni

SWEET SOY-BRAISED EGGPLANT

Gluten-Free, Nut-Free, Vegan

PREP TIME: 15 MINUTES | COOK TIME: 45 MINUTES | SERVES 4

Eggplant is one of my favorite vegetables. When cooked right, its flesh is soft, sweet, and lovingly takes on the flavors of the sauce you're cooking it in. The trick to this simple side dish is to thoroughly allow the oil to soak into the eggplant before adding the water. This will make the eggplant taste richer and prevent it from falling apart when it's simmering in the sauce. This dish improves as it rests in the days that follow and can be eaten cold.

---

4 Japanese or Chinese eggplants (about 1 pound)

3 tablespoons avocado oil, divided

1 tablespoon sugar

2½ tablespoons soy sauce or tamari

1. Trim the ends of the eggplants and cut them in half lengthwise. Place the eggplant halves, cut-side down, on the cutting board and make tiny slits, about ⅛ inch apart, down the length of the eggplant on a diagonal, but not cutting all the way through.

2. Heat 1½ tablespoons avocado oil in a large pot over medium heat. Add half of the eggplants, skin-side down, and cook for about 1 minute.

3. Once the skin side has softened a bit, flip and rotate the position of the eggplants. Let them cook until the oil has been absorbed, 10 to 15 minutes. Transfer the eggplants to a plate and repeat with the remaining oil and eggplants. The eggplants shouldn't be completely cooked through at this point.

4. Put all the eggplants back in the pot—it's fine if they don't all fit in a single layer. Pour in enough water so that the eggplants are mostly covered but still peeking out a bit. Add the sugar and bring to a boil.

5. Cut a piece of aluminum foil to fit inside your pot. Press the foil down into the pot so that it sits on the surface of the eggplants. Continue cooking for 5 minutes.

6. Add the soy sauce and stir, changing the position of the eggplants to get even cooking. Continue to cook, occasionally basting with the sauce, until the eggplants are completely soft, about 15 minutes. Serve.

GARLICKY SHOYU POBLANOS

Gluten-Free, Nut-Free, 30 Minutes or Less, Vegan

PREP TIME: 20 MINUTES | COOK TIME: 10 MINUTES | MAKES ABOUT 1 CUP

The inspiration for this recipe came from my husband's spunky aunt. She loves Mexican food, and I think this dish marries the two cuisines beautifully. Auntie Jackie makes this with jalapeños, which give it a nice kick. If that's more your style, replace some or all of the poblanos with jalapeños or experiment with a different pepper altogether. This dish is a small side and is meant to accompany rice as a part of a larger meal.

3 poblano peppers, stemmed, seeded, and halved lengthwise

2 tablespoons olive oil

1 tablespoon soy sauce or tamari

1 garlic clove, grated

1. Preheat the broiler to high and position a rack as close to the heating element as possible. Set aside a medium bowl and a plate that can fit on top of it like a lid.

2. Place the peppers, skin-side up, in a single row down the center of a rimmed baking sheet. You may have to work in batches if the peppers don't all fit on one sheet.

3. Broil until blackened, about 4 minutes, moving the baking sheet as necessary to ensure an even char.

4. Immediately place the blackened peppers in the bowl and cover with the plate.

5. When the peppers are cool enough to handle, slip the skins off with your fingers. Cut the peppers crosswise into ½-inch strips.

6. In a bowl, mix the peppers, olive oil, soy sauce, and garlic until well coated. Serve.

PREP TIP: If you have a gas burner, the peppers can also be blackened over the stove. With a pair of tongs, rest the whole pepper on the burner over medium heat until it blackens. Rotate until all sides and crevices are blistered, then continue the recipe, beginning with step 4.

ROASTED PEPPERS IN DASHI SAUCE

Gluten-Free, Nut-Free, Vegan

PREP TIME: 10 MINUTES | COOK TIME: 5 MINUTES | MARINATE TIME: 2 HOURS | SERVES 4

The peppers in this dish are typically deep-fried before being added to the sauce. In an effort to avoid the trouble and mess, this recipe is similar to Garlicky Shoyu Poblanos (page 59) in concept but very different in flavor. In this case, the dashi sauce is sweeter and mild. If I have a batch of either in the refrigerator, a quick meal can be made when served along with rice, eggs, and Miso Soup (page 20).

2 red bell peppers, halved lengthwise, cored, and seeded

1 jalapeño, halved lengthwise, cored, and seeded

½ cup Basic Dashi (page 18) or Vegan Dashi (page 19)

2 tablespoons Sweet Soy Concentrate (page 28)

2 tablespoons olive oil

1. Preheat the broiler to high and position a rack as close to the heating element as possible. Set aside a medium bowl and a plate that can fit on top of it like a lid.

2. Place the bell peppers and jalapeño, skin-side up, in a single row down the center of a rimmed baking sheet.

3. Broil until blackened, about 5 minutes, moving the baking sheet as necessary to ensure an even char.

4. Immediately place the blackened peppers in the bowl and cover with the plate.

5. When the peppers are cool enough to handle, slip the skins off with your fingers. Cut the peppers into ½-inch strips.

6. Gently heat the dashi and sweet soy concentrate in a small pot over medium-low heat until warmed through.

7. Pour the dashi sauce into a jar or container and add the olive oil. Add the peppers and let cool.

8. Cover and store in the refrigerator to let the flavors meld for at least 2 hours. The peppers can be eaten cold or at room temperature.

PREP TIP: See the Prep Tip in the recipe for Garlicky Shoyu Poblanos (page 59) for instructions on how to char peppers using a gas burner.

VARIATION TIP: Depending on the season, you could also use onion, eggplant, kabocha, and asparagus.

Kinpira Gobō

SWEET STIR-FRIED CARROTS AND BURDOCK ROOT

Gluten-Free, Nut-Free, 30 Minutes or Less, Vegan

PREP TIME: 15 MINUTES **|** COOK TIME: 10 MINUTES **|** SERVES 4

I didn't care much for burdock root as a kid, but I've come to love its distinct woody texture and earthy flavor. Burdock root can be stir-fried, deep-fried, or stewed, and because its flavor is mild, it takes on the flavors of whatever you're cooking it with. At Asian markets, it comes in a long plastic sleeve about 2 feet long. I've also seen it at Whole Foods in shorter pieces, about the length of a cucumber.

1 (12-inch) piece burdock root

1 medium carrot, peeled

1 teaspoon toasted sesame oil

4 tablespoons water (optional, if needed)

1 tablespoon soy sauce or tamari

1 tablespoon mirin

Small pinch red pepper flakes (optional)

1. Cut the burdock root in half crosswise to make it more manageable. Peel, then thinly slice the root on a sharp diagonal. Stack the burdock slices and julienne. Soak the pieces in a bowl of water.

2. Julienne the carrot in the same way as the burdock root and set aside. (Note: The carrot does not need to soak.)

3. Heat the sesame oil in a large skillet over medium heat. Drain the burdock almost completely and add it to the pan. (A little bit of remaining water helps steam the burdock root as it cooks.) Stir-fry until the burdock softens a little, about 5 minutes.

4. Add the carrots to the pan and stir-fry until the carrots are cooked through, about 3 minutes. If the pan is dry, add the water, a couple of tablespoons at a time.

5. Add the soy sauce, mirin, and red pepper flakes (if using) and continue to stir-fry until most of the liquid has cooked off and the vegetables are coated with the sauce, about 2 minutes. Serve.

VARIATION TIP: You can also use other vegetables, like kabocha squash (cut into matchsticks) or lotus root (cut into thin quarter moons). Or try parsnip (julienned), but reduce the mirin to 2 teaspoons.

Hakusai No Itamemono

STIR-FRIED NAPA CABBAGE WITH GINGER

Gluten-Free, Nut-Free, 30 Minutes or Less, Vegan

PREP TIME: 10 MINUTES | COOK TIME: 15 MINUTES | SERVES 4

Rarely does a recipe call for a whole napa cabbage. So after you've used half a cabbage for Pork and Cabbage Pot Stickers (page 119) or Hot Pot with Black Cod and Mushrooms (page 96), try this simple dish. The splash of vinegar and the flavor of the ginger perfectly highlight the sweetness of the cabbage.

1 teaspoon potato starch or cornstarch

1 teaspoon water

½ small napa cabbage

4 tablespoons avocado oil, divided

Heaping ¼ teaspoon salt

1 (1-inch) piece ginger, peeled and cut into ⅛-inch slices

1 tablespoon soy sauce or tamari

1 teaspoon rice vinegar

1. In a small bowl, stir together the potato starch and water and set aside.

2. Cut the cabbage half crosswise into 1½-inch sections. Separate the white stems from the leafy light green ends.

3. In a large skillet, heat 3 tablespoons avocado oil over medium-high heat. When the oil is hot, add the white cabbage stems and stir-fry until translucent, about 6 minutes.

4. Add the leafy greens and stir to coat with oil. Add the salt and stir to combine. Stir-fry until the cabbage is soft and the moisture has released, about 5 minutes. If the cabbage is watery, place it in a fine-mesh strainer to drain. If not, set it aside on a large plate.

5. Heat the remaining 1 tablespoon oil in the same pan over medium heat. Add the ginger and cook until fragrant, about 1 minute. Add the soy sauce and vinegar, then return the cabbage to the pan and stir to incorporate well.

6. Once combined, take the small bowl with the potato starch mixture and stir with your finger to mix the slurry before drizzling over the cabbage. Moving quickly, incorporate and cook just until the sauce has thickened. Serve.

CAULIFLOWER STEAK WITH MISO-HONEY BUTTER

Gluten-Free, Nut-Free, Vegetarian

PREP TIME: 20 MINUTES | COOK TIME: 40 MINUTES | SERVES 4

I had to test this recipe a few times to get the baking temperature and timing right, but both times my daughter excitedly dug in. Using 2 teaspoons of honey was on the sweet side for my husband and me but not my daughter. Be sure to taste the marinade and adjust the seasoning, since the saltiness of miso can vary quite a bit. Serve along with Hamburger Steak (page 112) and rice.

2 tablespoons unsalted butter

1 tablespoon miso

2 teaspoons honey

1 garlic clove, grated

1 head cauliflower

1. Preheat the oven to 425°F. Line a rimmed baking sheet with parchment paper.

2. Gently heat the butter in a small pot over low heat. Once melted, remove from the heat and whisk in the miso, honey, and garlic.

3. Cut the cauliflower in half vertically through the core. Take one half of the cauliflower and make a 1-inch cut parallel to your previous cut. Place the cauliflower "steak" on the baking sheet and repeat with the other half. Place the leftover florets on the baking sheet too (cut very large florets in half).

4. Lightly brush the miso butter on both sides of the cauliflower steaks and on the florets.

5. Bake for 20 minutes. Brush both sides of the cauliflower steaks and the florets with the miso-honey butter again. Continue to bake until nicely browned, 15 to 20 more minutes.

Sukoppu Korokke

MASHED POTATO BAKE

Nut-Free, Vegetarian

PREP TIME: 30 MINUTES | COOK TIME: 30 MINUTES | SERVES 4

I went to junior high school in Tokyo, and along the route was a butcher. My friends and I would often order fried potato croquettes on our way home. The butcher placed our snack, drizzled with tonkatsu sauce, in a little paper envelope. We'd nibble on them, crisp and hot, on our way to the train station. This is a contemporary take, simplifying the recipe by baking it all in a dish instead of shaping, breading, and deep-frying individual croquettes.

---

1 cup panko breadcrumbs

1 pound russet potatoes, peeled and cut into 1-inch pieces

1 teaspoon avocado oil

½ onion, chopped

1 carrot, peeled and coarsely grated

½ cup frozen peas, thawed

4 teaspoons mirin

4 teaspoons milk, plus more if needed

Heaping ½ teaspoon salt

Pinch ground white pepper

1 tablespoon olive oil

Tonkatsu Sauce (page 29), for serving

1. Preheat the oven to 450°F.

2. Toast the panko in a dry skillet over medium heat, stirring constantly, until golden, about 4 minutes. Transfer to a plate to cool.

3. Pour an inch of water into a large pot. Cover and bring to a boil over medium-high heat. Put the potatoes in a metal steamer basket and place the basket in the pot. Cover the pot, reduce the heat to medium-low, and steam the potatoes until soft, 15 to 20 minutes.

4. Meanwhile, heat the avocado oil in a small skillet over medium heat. Add the onion and carrot and cook until softened, about 5 minutes. Set aside.

5. Transfer the potatoes to a large bowl. Mash the potatoes with a fork or masher. Add the cooked onions and carrots, the peas, mirin, milk, salt, and pepper and mix with a spatula or wooden spoon. If the mixture is dry, add more milk until it is moist like mashed potatoes. Taste and adjust the seasonings as necessary.

6. Scoop the potatoes into a small baking dish or pie plate, spreading them into an even layer. Top with the panko, drizzle evenly with the olive oil, and bake for 7 minutes.

7. Scoop onto individual plates and serve drizzled with tonkatsu sauce.

> **VARIATION TIP:** If you want to make this dish creamier, incorporate shredded cheese into the potato mixture. Crushed cornflakes are a good gluten-free alternative for the panko topping.

CHAPTER FIVE

RICE AND NOODLES

BACON FRIED RICE

Gluten-Free, Nut-Free, 30 Minutes or Less

PREP TIME: 10 MINUTES | COOK TIME: 20 MINUTES | SERVES 4

Fried rice is the perfect way to use leftover rice. It's a good dish to have in your arsenal because it can make a satisfying meal out of any vegetable or meat you have sitting in the fridge. Once you understand the basic concept—fry the aromatics, add the vegetables/meat and rice, scramble the egg, and season—you'll be able to riff on this recipe in endless ways. Refrigerating the rice for 2 days may seem weirdly specific, but the rice hardens during that time. This helps maintain the integrity of the grains so the final dish won't be mushy.

---

2 large eggs

¼ teaspoon toasted sesame oil

Salt

Freshly ground black pepper

4 bacon slices, cut into ½-inch pieces

½ onion, chopped

¼ teaspoon grated ginger

1 recipe Basic Short-Grain Rice (page 16), refrigerated for 2 days

2 teaspoons sake

1½ teaspoons soy sauce or tamari

8 shiso leaves, thinly sliced

1. Crack the eggs in a small bowl, add the sesame oil and a pinch each of salt and pepper, and whisk well. Set aside.

2. Heat a wok or large skillet over medium heat. Add the bacon and fry until crispy, 3 to 5 minutes. Use a slotted spoon to transfer the bacon to a paper towel–lined plate, leaving the drippings in the pan.

3. Keeping the heat at medium, add the onion and ginger and cook until fragrant, about 3 to 5 minutes. Increase the heat to high and add the rice, breaking up any clumps with the back of a wooden spoon, and continue stirring for a couple of minutes or until everything is incorporated.

4. Add the cooked bacon and toss to mix. Make a well in the center of the ingredients in the pan. Pour the egg into it and scramble. Stir to combine everything together.

5. Add the sake and soy sauce, then taste and season with salt and pepper, as needed. Stir until evenly combined. Turn off the heat, mix in the shiso leaves, and serve.

> **VARIATION TIP:** If you can't find shiso, an equal mix of mint and basil is a good substitute.

MIXED RICE WITH PORK AND BAMBOO SHOOTS

Gluten-Free, Nut-Free, 30 Minutes or Less

PREP TIME: 10 MINUTES | COOK TIME: 10 MINUTES

Maze gohan translates to "mixed rice," a method of mixing ingredients into rice that has already been cooked. I had always assumed that takikomi gohan, where the ingredients are cooked in the same pot at the same time as the rice, would leave the rice infused with flavor, and therefore be better. This recipe proved my assumptions wrong. This maze gohan is flavorful and texturally interesting because of the bamboo shoots.

---

1 tablespoon avocado oil

8 ounces ground pork

1 (8-ounce) can bamboo shoots, drained and diced

2 tablespoons plus 1 teaspoon soy sauce or tamari

1½ tablespoons mirin

1¼ teaspoons sake

¾ teaspoon sugar

1 recipe Basic Short-Grain Rice (page 16)

Freshly ground black pepper

1. Heat the oil in a medium skillet over medium heat. Add the pork and cook until the meat is no longer pink, about 3 minutes. Add the bamboo shoots and cook for a minute or two.

2. Add the soy sauce, mirin, sake, and sugar and cook, stirring occasionally, until there is only a little liquid left in the pan, 5 to 7 minutes.

3. Scrape the pork mixture into a large bowl. Add the hot rice and gently fold in the ingredients until combined. Do not overmix. Season with black pepper and serve.

> **VARIATION TIP:** You can also use fresh bamboo shoots for this recipe or, if bamboo shoots are unavailable, you can substitute coarsely grated burdock root or chopped green cabbage. Cook the burdock root or cabbage until softened, about 5 minutes.

Omuraisu

EASY OMELET RICE

Gluten-Free, Nut-Free, 30 Minutes or Less

PREP TIME: 10 MINUTES | COOK TIME: 15 MINUTES | SERVES 4

Omuraisu evokes nostalgia and comfort and is right up there with curry as one of Japan's classic childhood foods. It takes practice and deft skill to make the traditional omelet; if you're feeling ambitious, try your hand using the tip on the next page. Here, I'm offering a little cheat, with soft scrambled eggs spooned on top of the rice instead. Additional ingredients can be added at the beginning with the chicken and onion, such as diced carrots, corn, and mushrooms.

---

2 tablespoons unsalted butter, divided

1 boneless, skinless chicken thigh, cut into small pieces

½ onion, chopped

½ cup frozen green peas, thawed

¼ cup ketchup, plus more for serving

1 recipe Basic Short-Grain Rice (page 16)

Salt

Freshly ground black pepper

8 large eggs

¼ cup milk

1. Melt 1 tablespoon butter in a large skillet over medium heat. Add the chicken and onion and cook until the chicken is no longer pink and the onion is translucent, about 5 minutes.

2. Add the peas and ketchup and cook, stirring constantly, until the moisture from the ketchup has evaporated and the mixture looks dry, about 2 minutes.

3. Add the hot rice and season with a couple pinches of salt and pepper. Very gently mix everything together using a slicing motion, flipping the rice from bottom to top. Be careful not to smash the grains of rice or it will turn mushy.

4. Pack 4 small bowls with the rice. Place a plate on top each bowl, then flip it upside down. Keep the bowls in place to keep the rice warm while you make the eggs.

5. Heat a large nonstick skillet over medium-low heat for about 3 minutes. Meanwhile, in a small bowl, whisk the eggs with the milk and a pinch of salt.

6. Add the remaining 1 tablespoon butter to the pan and swirl until melted. Add the eggs and scramble to your desired doneness, paying close attention to turn the heat off just before they are fully cooked.

7. Remove the bowls to uncover the rice, and spoon the eggs over the rice. Squirt some ketchup over the eggs and serve.

PREP TIP: To make this as a traditional omuraisu, you won't have to portion out the rice onto plates as described in step 4. Instead, make the dish one serving at a time, using 2 eggs per serving. Add the eggs to a heated small nonstick pan. Cook as you would a traditional omelet and add a quarter of the rice in the center, wrapping the egg around the rice before plating.

Kinoko Gohan

MIXED RICE WITH MUSHROOMS AND GINGER

Gluten-Free, Nut-Free, Vegan

PREP TIME: 30 MINUTES | COOK TIME: 35 MINUTES | SERVES 4

This dish is a hybrid of a takikomi gohan ("cooked with rice") and a maze gohan ("mixed in rice after cooked") recipe. The mushrooms are cooked on the stove, then the liquid and the juices from the mushrooms are used to cook the rice. It's the best of both worlds because you can control the doneness of the mushrooms and cook a flavorful rice. If you like, replace the beech mushrooms with oyster, maitake, or king trumpet mushrooms. If aburaage is hard to find, finely dice half a boneless, skinless chicken thigh or omit altogether.

1½ cups short-grain white rice

1 piece aburaage

¾ cup Basic Dashi (page 18) or Vegan Dashi (page 19)

3 tablespoons soy sauce or tamari

1 tablespoon sake

1 tablespoon mirin

2 teaspoons sugar

1 (3.5-ounce) package beech mushrooms, trimmed and separated by hand

6 fresh shiitake mushrooms, stemmed and cut into ⅓-inch pieces

1 (1-inch) piece ginger, peeled and sliced crosswise into ⅛-inch rounds

Pinch salt

1. Wash and drain the rice according to the directions on page 16, up to step 7. Leave the rice to drain in a fine-mesh strainer while you prepare the other ingredients.

2. Wrap the aburaage in a paper towel and run a rolling pin over it to extract the excess oil. Cut it into ¼-inch squares.

3. In a medium pot, combine the dashi, soy sauce, sake, mirin, sugar, mushrooms, ginger, and aburaage. Bring to a boil over medium heat, reduce the heat to medium-low, and cook for 2 to 3 minutes. Using a fine-mesh strainer, strain into a 2-cup or larger measuring cup. Reserve the mushrooms and discard the ginger.

4. Put the rice in a small pot. Pour water into the measuring cup with the dashi mixture until you have a little more than 1½ cups of liquid. Add the liquid to the pot with the salt and stir.

5. Bring the pot to a boil over medium heat. Cover, reduce the heat to low, and cook for 20 minutes.

6. When the rice has finished cooking, add the mushrooms to the pot. Cover immediately and let the mixture sit for 8 minutes.

7. Gently fold in the mushrooms with a rice paddle or fork, being careful not to crush the grains of rice. Serve.

> **PREP TIP:** To use a rice cooker for this recipe, put the rice in the rice cooker and add the dashi mixture and enough water for the amount of rice. Stir in a pinch of salt. Start the rice cooker, then continue on to step 6.

Takikomi Gohan

VEGETABLES COOKED WITH RICE

Gluten-Free, Nut-Free

PREP TIME: 30 MINUTES | COOK TIME: 30 MINUTES | SERVES 4

Takikomi translates to "cooked with," meaning the vegetables are cooked along with the rice. This dish is gently seasoned and is a great accompaniment to main dishes like Miso-Marinated Salmon (page 94), Clear Mushroom Soup (page 21), and Easy Cucumber Pickles (page 35). The ingredients with the rice can vary: bamboo shoots, burdock root, minced chicken, etc. What I like about this particular combination of ingredients is that I usually have them on hand, regardless of the season.

1½ cups short-grain white rice

1 dried shiitake mushroom

½ piece aburaage

2 tablespoons soy sauce or tamari

2 tablespoons mirin

1 tablespoon sake

2 pinches salt

½ carrot, minced

2 teaspoons bonito flakes, rubbed to break up the flakes

1. Wash and drain the rice according to the direction on page 16, up to step 7. Then drain in a fine-mesh strainer while you prepare the other ingredients.

2. Put the shiitake mushroom in a small bowl and pour in enough water to cover it. Soak for about 20 minutes. Drain, but save the soaking liquid. Mince the shiitake.

3. Wrap the aburaage in a paper towel and run a rolling pin over it to extract the excess oil. Mince the aburaage.

4. Combine the soy sauce, mirin, sake, shiitake-soaking liquid, and salt in a measuring cup and add water until it measures to a little over 1½ cups.

5. Combine the rice and liquid in a small pot. Place the carrot, aburaage, shiitake, and bonito flakes on top of the rice. Do not stir. Bring to a boil over medium heat. Cover, reduce the heat to low, and cook for 20 minutes. After the cooking time is completed, turn off the heat and let the mixture sit for 10 minutes.

6. Once the rice is done, gently fluff and fold the ingredients together with a rice paddle or fork, being careful not to crush the grains of rice. Serve.

PREP TIP: To use a rice cooker for this dish, put the rice in the rice cooker and add the soy sauce mixture and enough water for the amount of rice. Place the carrot, aburaage, shiitake, and bonito flakes on top of the rice. Do not stir. Start the rice cooker.

Inarizushi

FOOTBALL SUSHI

Freezer Friendly, Gluten-Free, Nut-Free, Vegan

PREP TIME: 45 MINUTES | COOK TIME: 20 MINUTES | MAKES 10 PIECES

You can often find inarizushi—or football sushi, as it is often called in the Japanese-American community because of how it looks—at gatherings and pot-lucks. You can make the pouches a day in advance or freeze them for a later use.

---

5 pieces aburaage

1¼ cups Basic Dashi (page 18) or Vegan Dashi (page 19)

2 tablespoons soy sauce or tamari

2 tablespoons sugar

1½ tablespoons mirin

1 recipe Basic Short-Grain Rice (page 16)

6 tablespoons Sushi Vinegar (page 27)

Toasted sesame seeds

1. Fold a paper towel in half and place one aburaage inside. Press with a rolling pin to release any excess oil. Repeat with the remaining aburaage, then cut all of them in half crosswise.

2. Combine the dashi, soy sauce, sugar, and mirin in a medium pot and stir over medium heat until the sugar is dissolved.

3. Add the aburaage and bring to a boil. Reduce the heat to medium-low. Cut a piece of aluminum foil to fit inside your pot and press the foil down into the pot so that it sits on the surface of the aburaage. Cook for 4 minutes.

4. Remove the foil. The soft aburaage will tear easily so gently turn them over for even cooking. Increase the heat to medium and continue cooking until most of the liquid has reduced, 10 to 15 minutes. Turn off the heat and let the mixture cool.

5. Put the cooked rice in a large, wide bowl. Slowly pour the sushi vinegar evenly over the rice and mix quickly but gently, alternately using a slicing motion and scooping then flipping the rice from bottom to top.

6. Once it looks like the grains have been coated in the vinegar, sprinkle with the sesame seeds and cool by waving a hand fan or stiff piece of paper over the rice (see Prep Tip). Occasionally slice, scoop, and flip the rice to allow it to cool evenly.

7. Gently squeeze the aburaage and carefully open up the cut side to create a pocket. With wet hands, place a small portion of rice in your palm and squeeze gently to form an oval-shaped orb.

8. Insert the orb of rice into the aburaage and add more rice, if needed, to fill to about three-quarters full. Fold one side of the pocket down against the rice and fold the other side on top. Place the sushi fold-side down for serving.

> **PREP TIP:** Uchiwa hand fans are common in every Japanese household and are used to cool the rice once the vinegar has been mixed in. You can wave a piece of cardboard or stiff piece of paper instead. It'll be tempting to stick it in the refrigerator or freezer, but I don't recommend this.

Chirashizushi

MIXED-VEGETABLE SUSHI RICE

Gluten-Free, Nut-Free, Vegetarian
PREP TIME: 45 MINUTES | COOK TIME: 20 MINUTES | SERVES 4

With its bright colors, chirashizushi feels celebratory and fun. It's one of the more advanced recipes in this book, but keep in mind that the vegetables, vinegar, and toppings can be prepped a day ahead so you can simply cook the rice and mix everything together before serving. You can use other seasonal vegetables instead of the snow peas, such as green beans or asparagus. If you can't find shiso, an equal mix of mint and basil is a good substitute. Serve alongside Japanese "Fried" Chicken (page 118) and Clear Mushroom Soup (page 21).

---

3 dried shiitake
   mushrooms

10 snow pea pods

¼ carrot, peeled,
   quartered lengthwise,
   then thinly sliced
   crosswise

2 ounces fresh or canned
   bamboo shoots, sliced
   into thin pieces

¾ cup Basic Dashi
   (page 18) or Vegan
   Dashi (page 19)

1½ tablespoons sugar

2 tablespoons soy sauce
   or tamari

1 recipe Basic Short-Grain
   Rice (page 16)

6 tablespoons Sushi
   Vinegar (page 27)

1 teaspoon avocado oil

2 large eggs, beaten

4 shiso leaves, thinly
   sliced, for garnish

1. Put the shiitakes in a small bowl, add water to cover, and soak for 30 minutes. Drain, then mince.

2. Meanwhile, bring a small pot of water to a boil over medium-high heat. Add the snow peas and blanch for 1 minute, then drain and run under cool water. Pat dry and thinly slice on a diagonal and set aside.

3. Combine the shiitake, carrot, and bamboo shoots in a small pot. Add the dashi and sugar. Bring to a boil over medium-high heat, then reduce to a moderate simmer.

4. Cut a piece of aluminum foil to fit inside your pot and press the foil down into the pot so that it sits on the surface of the vegetables. Cook for 5 minutes. Remove and discard the foil, and add the soy sauce and cook over medium-low to low heat until the liquid reduces, about 10 minutes.

5. Put the cooked rice in a large, wide bowl. Slowly pour the sushi vinegar evenly over the rice and mix quickly but gently, alternately using a slicing motion and scooping then flipping the rice from bottom to top. Once it looks like the grains have been coated in the vinegar, begin to cool the rice by waving a hand fan or stiff piece of paper over the rice (see Prep Tip on page 77).

6. When the rice is no longer steaming but still warm, add the vegetables and any remaining liquid to the rice. Gently incorporate the ingredients as before but do not overmix. Continue to fan for a couple of minutes, then set aside to cool to room temperature. Occasionally slice, scoop, and flip the rice to allow it to cool evenly.

7. Heat the oil in a small nonstick skillet over medium heat. When it is hot, wipe the excess oil from the pan with a paper towel and set the paper towel aside.

8. Pour some of the beaten eggs into the pan and turn to evenly coat the bottom of the pan so you have a thin layer of egg. Lower the heat to medium-low. Once the egg is cooked but still looks glossy on the surface, about 1 minute, use chopsticks or a rubber spatula to gently flip. Allow the egg to finish cooking for a few seconds. Place the egg on a cutting board to cool. Use the paper towel you set aside earlier to rub a little oil onto the pan and repeat with the remaining beaten eggs.

9. Once cool, stack the cooked eggs and slice them in half and then in quarters. Roll each piece into a log and thinly slice.

10. Top the rice with the shiso, then scatter the egg and snow peas evenly across the surface. Serve.

TUNA CHIRASHI WITH SNOW PEAS

Gluten-Free, Nut-Free, 30 Minutes or Less

PREP TIME: 20 MINUTES | COOK TIME: 5 MINUTES | SERVES 4

In this version of chirashi, cooked vegetables and fish are mixed in with sushi rice. The combination of the vinegary rice and curried canned tuna gives a wonderfully sweet and tangy flavor. Pair with Miso Soup (page 20) and a vegetable side like Spinach Dressed with Tofu (page 48).

1 recipe Basic Short-Grain Rice (page 16)

6 tablespoons Sushi Vinegar (page 27)

30 snow pea pods

2 (5-ounce) cans solid tuna packed in oil, drained

1 teaspoon curry powder

2 teaspoons soy sauce or tamari

Salt

Freshly ground black pepper

1. Put the cooked rice in a large, wide bowl. Slowly pour the sushi vinegar evenly over the rice and mix quickly but gently, alternately using a slicing motion and scooping then flipping the rice from bottom to top.

2. Once it looks like the grains have been coated in the vinegar, cool the rice by waving a hand fan or stiff piece of paper over the rice (see Prep Tip on page 77). Set aside to cool to room temperature. Occasionally slice, scoop, and flip the rice to allow it to cool evenly.

3. Meanwhile, bring a small pot of water to a boil over medium-high heat. Add the snow peas and blanch for 1 minute, then drain and run under cool water. Slice on the diagonal into ½-inch pieces. Set aside.

4. Put the tuna in a small skillet and cook over medium heat, breaking it up into small flakes with the back of a wooden spoon. Add the curry powder, soy sauce, and a pinch each of salt and pepper. Mix and cook until well combined, about 3 minutes.

5. Add the tuna to the rice. Mix gently until incorporated, then fold in the snow peas. Serve.

Yakisoba

PORK BELLY PANFRIED NOODLES

Nut-Free, 30 Minutes or Less

PREP TIME: 20 MINUTES | COOK TIME: 10 MINUTES | SERVES 3

Yakisoba is the food of my childhood. It's a panfried noodle tossed with vegetables and a little meat and tastes savory and slightly sweet. I associate it with crowded street festivals, humid carefree summers, and epic fireworks. It's street food but it's also common to make at home. To make it meatless, scramble or fry an egg at the end to replace the meat. Traditionally, this dish is topped with aonori seaweed and benishoga (pickled ginger), and they add nice accents if you can find them.

---

3 tablespoons sake

1½ tablespoons ketchup

1½ tablespoons Worcestershire sauce

1½ tablespoons oyster sauce

1½ teaspoons sugar

1½ teaspoons avocado oil

12 ounces frozen pork belly, thawed for 30 minutes and thinly sliced

½ small onion, cut into ½-inch slices

3 cabbage leaves, cut into ½-inch-wide ribbons

1 small carrot, julienned

1 (1-pound) package refrigerated yakisoba noodles

6 tablespoons water

1. In a small bowl, whisk together the sake, ketchup, Worcestershire sauce, oyster sauce, and sugar until the sugar has dissolved.

2. Heat the oil in a large skillet over medium heat. Add the pork and cook until no longer pink, about 3 minutes. Add the onion, cabbage, and carrot and cook until softened, about 3 minutes.

3. Make a well in the center of your pan. Add the noodles and drizzle the water evenly over them. Allow to cook for 1 minute undisturbed, then carefully flip the noodles over. They will start loosening and breaking apart. Help them along by wiggling chopsticks or a pasta server between them at various points.

4. Pour the sauce over the pan, then mix everything together until evenly coated. Serve.

> **VARIATION TIP:** Pork belly is traditional but feel free to use whatever meat you have on hand, such as bacon or chicken.

COLD NOODLES WITH OKRA, TOMATO, AND EGG

Nut-Free, 30 Minutes or Less, Vegetarian

PREP TIME: 20 MINUTES | COOK TIME: 20 MINUTES | SERVES 4

Traditionally, there is kake udon/soba—where the noodles sit in a hot broth—and zaru udon/soba—where the noodles are served separately and dipped in a concentrated cold broth to eat. This bukkake dish is a hybrid: A cold broth is poured over the noodles and served with various toppings. I had frozen udon noodles on hand, but dried, fresh, or frozen udon or soba noodles all work great here. The use of fried shallots is not at all conventional. I use it in place of fried tempura bits because I like the flavor it adds. Although each topping adds to the dish, if you are missing one or two elements, don't sweat it.

1½ cups Basic Dashi (page 18) or Vegan Dashi (page 19)

6 tablespoons Sweet Soy Concentrate (page 28)

4 okra

½ cup avocado oil

4 shallots, thinly sliced

2 pounds frozen udon (see Ingredient Tip)

1 pint cherry tomatoes, halved

4 soft-boiled eggs, halved

1 scallion, white and green parts, chopped

½ sheet nori, torn into small pieces

1. Stir together the dashi and sweet soy concentrate in a medium bowl or combine in a mason jar, cover, and refrigerate.

2. Bring a large pot of water to a boil over medium-high heat for the noodles.

3. Meanwhile, bring a small pot of water to a boil over medium-high heat. Add the okra and cook for 3 minutes, then drain and run under cool water. Thinly slice crosswise, then set aside.

4. Heat the oil in a small skillet over medium heat. Add the shallots (they should be fairly crowded so they will brown well) and cook, stirring occasionally, until golden, 8 to 10 minutes. Remove from the pan with a slotted spoon, place on a paper towel–lined plate, and set aside.

5. Cook the noodles according to the package directions. Drain and rinse with cold water. Once cool enough to handle, rub the noodles under running water to remove any excess starch. Drain well.

6. Divide the noodles among 4 serving bowls, pour the sauce equally into each bowl, and top with the okra, cherry tomatoes, eggs, scallion, fried shallots, and nori. Mix well and serve.

INGREDIENT TIP: Udon and soba not only vary in weight from each other, but they vary in weight depending on the brand and whether you use dried, fresh, or frozen noodles. I suggest serving 4 portions as given on the package you choose.

VARIATION TIP: If making this gluten free, use tamari and soba noodles made with buckwheat as their only ingredient (most brands use a combination of buckwheat and wheat).

Kitsune Udon/Soba

NOODLES WITH FRIED TOFU IN WARM BROTH

Nut-Free, 30 Minutes or Less, Vegan

PREP TIME: 5 MINUTES | COOK TIME: 25 MINUTES | SERVES 4

This is a very basic noodle dish. Once you know how to make this, you can try other variations like adding tempura or leftover chicken from Ground Chicken and Scrambled Egg Bowl (page 114) or Slow Cooker Shoyu Chicken (page 115). If you can't find aburaage, you can still make a satisfying meal by topping your noodles with these leftover meats or a soft-boiled egg, some steamed spinach, and scallions. This recipe is delicious with udon or soba noodles. See the Ingredient Tip about using different types of udon or soba.

5 cups Basic Dashi (page 18) or Vegan Dashi (page 19), divided

6 tablespoons Sweet Soy Concentrate (page 28)

4 pieces aburaage

¼ cup sugar

2 tablespoons soy sauce or tamari

2 pounds frozen udon (see Ingredient Tip)

2 scallions, white and green parts, thinly sliced, for garnish

1. Bring a large pot of water to a boil over medium-high heat for the noodles.

2. In a medium pot, gently heat 3½ cups dashi and the sweet soy concentrate.

3. In the meantime, fold a paper towel in half and place a piece of aburaage inside. Press with a rolling pin to release any excess oil. Repeat with the remaining aburaage.

4. Combine the remaining 1½ cups dashi, the sugar, and soy sauce in a small pot and bring to a boil over medium heat. Add the aburaage. Cut a piece of aluminum foil to fit inside your pot and press the foil down so that it sits on the surface of the aburaage. Reduce the heat to low and cook for 15 minutes. Uncover and flip the aburaage, so they will soak in the liquid evenly. Set aside to cool.

5. Boil the noodles according to the package directions. Drain and portion the noodles into individual bowls. Add the soup and aburaage and top with the scallions.

INGREDIENT TIP: Udon and soba not only vary in weight from each other, but they vary in weight depending on the brand and whether you use dried, fresh, or frozen noodles. I suggest serving 4 portions as given on the package you choose.

VARIATION TIP: Some of my favorite additional toppings include shichimi pepper, wakame, a soft-boiled egg, steamed spinach, and kamaboko fish cake. Feel free to experiment to find your own favorites. If making this gluten-free, use tamari and soba noodles made with buckwheat as their only ingredient (most brands use a combination of buckwheat and wheat).

TO SLURP OR NOT TO SLURP

Let's talk about how to eat noodles. In Japan, noodles are meant to be slurped in order to fully enjoy them. It doesn't matter what type of noodle it is—udon, soba, somen, ramen, yakisoba, and even spaghetti. In Japan, you slurp.

While it might seem odd or rude from an American perspective, there is a reason behind it. When you slurp, you incorporate air into your bite. Think of it like a wine tasting, where you take a sip of wine and aspirate it by pursing your lips and inhaling through your mouth. This technique helps access the full flavor. It takes practice to eat this way without splattering, but it can be fun. Give it a try!

SUPER SIMPLE RAMEN

Nut-Free, 30 Minutes or Less

PREP TIME: 10 MINUTES | COOK TIME: 10 MINUTES | SERVES 1

Is there anything more comforting than a bowl of ramen? Making ramen from scratch at home is not common in Japan, but here's a simplified version that satisfies when the craving hits. Using dashi makes for a clean-tasting broth. You can substitute half the amount of dashi with low-sodium chicken broth to give it more body but decrease the amount of soy sauce if you do. I've made this for one serving because it's easier to portion out the seasonings for each bowl and increase the number of servings, as needed.

---

1 serving (5 ounces) fresh or frozen ramen noodles (see Ingredient Tip)

1½ cups Basic Dashi (page 18)

1 tablespoon Sweet Soy Concentrate (page 28)

2 teaspoons soy sauce

½ teaspoon oyster sauce

½ teaspoon toasted sesame oil

½ garlic clove, minced

Pinch ground white pepper

SUGGESTED TOPPINGS

Chopped scallions

Soft-boiled egg or Miso-Marinated Eggs (page 36)

Slow Cooker Shoyu Chicken (page 115) or meat of choice

Nori

Corn

1. Bring a large pot of water to a boil over medium-high heat. Add the noodles and cook according to the package directions. Drain very well.

2. While the noodles are cooking, heat the dashi in a small pot over medium heat until piping hot.

3. Combine the sweet soy concentrate, soy sauce, oyster sauce, sesame oil, garlic, and pepper in a bowl.

4. Pour the dashi into the bowl. Add the noodles and desired toppings and serve.

INGREDIENT TIP: If you don't have access to ramen noodles, here's a hack: Fill a large pot with water plus 1 tablespoon baking soda for every 4 cups of water. Bring the water to a boil over high heat. Add spaghetti or angel hair pasta and cook for 1½ times the cooking time called for on the package. Keep an eye on the pot, because it can boil over. The baking soda reacts with the noodles to make them springy.

CREAMY SHIITAKE AND BACON PASTA

Nut-Free

PREP TIME: 15 MINUTES | COOK TIME: 25 MINUTES | SERVES 4 TO 6

One of my favorite things to eat in Japan is Italian food. I dare not call it fusion food because it's a genre of food in Japan that is deserving of its own categorization. This dish is just the tip of the Japanese-Italian iceberg, and I include it here because the recipe is simple and the ingredients are fairly common. The dried shiitakes add so much flavor that I don't recommend replacing them altogether, but you can add whatever other mushrooms you'd like.

8 small dried shiitake mushrooms

2 tablespoons olive oil

2 garlic cloves, minced

4 strips of bacon, cut into ½-inch strips

1½ cups heavy cream

Salt

Freshly ground black pepper

1 pound pasta, such as fettucine

1. For the pasta, bring a large pot of water to a boil over medium-high heat.

2. Meanwhile, put the dried shiitakes in a medium bowl and pour in enough boiling water to cover them. Let them sit for 15 minutes, or until soft.

3. Remove the shiitakes from the water with a slotted spoon. When cool enough to handle, gently squeeze the liquid out of them. Trim the tough stems and slice the caps into ¼-inch strips.

4. Heat the olive oil in a medium skillet over medium-low heat. Add the garlic and cook until fragrant, about 1 minute. Add the bacon and shiitakes. Cook, stirring occasionally, until the bacon has slightly browned, 3 to 5 minutes.

5. Add the cream to the pan and bring to a simmer. Season with salt and pepper to your liking and continue to simmer for 15 minutes.

6. While the sauce is simmering, cook the pasta according to the package directions, minus 2 minutes. Drain, reserving about ½ cup of the cooking liquid.

7. Add the noodles to the pan and increase the heat to medium. Mix well, until each noodle is well coated, the sauce has thickened, and the pasta is al dente, 2 to 3 minutes. If the sauce is looking too thick, add the reserved cooking liquid, a couple tablespoons at a time, until it reaches your desired consistency. Serve.

CHAPTER SIX

SEAFOOD

Shiojyake

SALTED SALMON

Freezer Friendly, Gluten-Free, Nut-Free

PREP TIME: 10 MINUTES | MARINATE TIME: 24 HOURS | COOK TIME: 10 MINUTES | SERVES 6

This recipe features an easy, useful technique you can apply to any fish or meat to allow the salt to penetrate the flesh and not just sit on the outside. Since the flavors are simple, it can pair well with a variety of dishes, like Roasted Peppers in Dashi Sauce (page 60) and Mashed Potato Bake (page 64).

---

1 (1-pound) skin-on salmon fillet

2 teaspoons kosher salt, divided

1 lemon, cut into wedges, for serving

1. Place a paper towel on a cutting board and place the salmon on top, skin-side down. Place another paper towel on top of the salmon and press down to remove any excess moisture. Discard the paper towels.

2. Cut the salmon into 1-inch-wide fillets. Place the pieces, with the skin facing to one side, on a tray or plate.

3. Sprinkle all the pieces with 1 teaspoon salt. Flip the pieces over and do the same on the other side.

4. Cover the plate with plastic wrap and refrigerate the fish for at least 1 day to allow the salt to infuse the salmon.

5. When ready to eat, preheat the oven to 350°F.

6. Transfer the salmon pieces to a small baking dish and bake until the salmon is flaky, 7 to 8 minutes.

7. Serve with lemon wedges on the side.

> **PREP TIP:** If you're not going to eat all of the salmon, consider freezing a portion. After salting the salmon, individually wrap the extra fillets in small pieces of parchment paper, put them in a zip-top bag, and seal, pressing out the air. The day before you're ready to cook it, defrost the fillets in the refrigerator overnight.

FURIKAKE SALMON

Gluten-Free, Nut-Free, 30 Minutes or Less

PREP TIME: 5 MINUTES | COOK TIME: 10 MINUTES | SERVES 4

My first post-college job was at a museum, and I had the good fortune of traveling to Hawaii many times for work. On one particular trip, one by one, my colleagues and I got the flu. In true aloha spirit, a local planned a home-cooked meal for us. This memorable salmon was delivered to us, and I continue to make it to this day. Although I don't know its origin story, I see it as an example of how food takes root and evolves, no matter the geographical location.

---

1 (1-pound) salmon fillet

Kosher salt

¼ teaspoon wasabi (optional)

2 tablespoons mayonnaise

1 to 2 tablespoons aji nori furikake, depending on the thickness of the salmon

1. Preheat the oven to 350°F. Line a rimmed baking sheet with aluminum foil.

2. Cut the salmon into 4 portions and place them on the baking sheet. Sprinkle evenly and generously with kosher salt.

3. If using the wasabi, mix it into the mayonnaise in a small bowl. Spoon about 1½ teaspoons of the mayonnaise mixture on top of each salmon slice and spread to evenly coat the surface. There should be a nice layer of mayonnaise with none of the salmon peeking through.

4. Sprinkle enough furikake evenly over the mayonnaise on each salmon piece to cover the mayonnaise.

5. Bake until flaky, 7 to 10 minutes, depending on the thickness of your salmon.

INGREDIENT TIP: Furikakeru means "to shake over to cover," meaning a topping to sprinkle over rice. The aji nori flavor called for in this recipe and Furikake Popcorn (page 33) is made with white and black sesame seeds, seaweed, salt, sugar, and hydrolyzed soy protein.

MISO-MARINATED SALMON

Freezer-Friendly, Gluten-Free, Nut-Free

PREP TIME: 5 MINUTES | MARINATE TIME: 30 MINUTES | COOK TIME: 10 MINUTES | SERVES 4

While Salted Salmon (page 92) is the simplest way to cook fish, sometimes it's nice to have a more flavorful marinade. This marinade can be prepared, then placed in a zip-top bag with the salmon and stored in the freezer. Defrost overnight in the refrigerator the day before you want to cook it.

¼ cup sake

2 tablespoons miso

2 tablespoons honey

2 tablespoons minced garlic

½ teaspoon ginger juice, from squeezed grated ginger

1 (1-pound) salmon fillet, cut into 4 portions

1. Whisk together the sake, miso, honey, garlic, and ginger in a shallow dish. Add the salmon, cover, and refrigerate for at least 30 minutes or up to a few hours. Flip the salmon halfway through marinating.

2. Preheat the oven to 350°F.

3. Bake the salmon for 7 to 10 minutes, depending on the thickness of the fillets, until flaky.

SEAFOOD CENTERED

In Japan, seafood reigns. As an archipelago, Japan has access to abundant fish and seafood and has thrived on it for many years. Buddhism played some role in shaping the primarily seafood- and vegetable-focused diet, because killing land animals was not acceptable for a period of time.

At the world's largest wholesale seafood market in Tokyo, formerly known as Tsukiji Fish Market, I was fascinated by all the edible sea animals I had never seen before. Tourists come to watch the bidding on tuna and other fish early in the morning and eat sushi for breakfast afterward. In 2018, the inner market where the bidding took place moved to Toyosu Market, but the outer markets and shops remain at Tsukiji Market, where they sell kitchen goods, groceries, and other supplies.

DAIKON SIMMERED WITH MACKEREL

Gluten-Free, Nut-Free

PREP TIME: 5 MINUTES | COOK TIME: 1 HOUR | SERVES 4

Smaller, oily fish like salmon, sardines, and mackerel have been encouraged in the American diet to increase our consumption of omega-3s. I came up with this dish to use canned mackerel, since fresh is sometimes hard to find. I've also made this with tuna and it was just as delicious. Eat this as one of a few sides or use it to top a bowl of rice.

---

1 (1-pound) daikon, peeled, halved lengthwise, and cut crosswise into 1½-inch-thick pieces

1½ cups Basic Dashi (page 18)

2 tablespoons soy sauce or tamari, plus more if needed

2 tablespoons sake

2 tablespoons mirin

½ teaspoon sugar

1 (6-ounce) can boneless, skinless mackerel in oil, drained well

2 teaspoons potato starch or cornstarch

2 teaspoons water

1. Bring a large pot of water to a boil over medium-high heat. Cook the daikon for 10 minutes. Drain, then return to the pot.

2. Add the dashi and bring to a boil, then add the soy sauce, sake, mirin, and sugar. Reduce the heat to medium-low and cook for 40 minutes, stirring occasionally.

3. Add the mackerel and roughly break up the fish with a wooden spoon. Cook until warmed through, about 5 minutes. Reduce the heat to low.

4. In a small bowl, whisk together the potato starch and water. Stir to dissolve, then drizzle the slurry into the pot. Stir well, increase the heat to medium, and cook until the sauce has thickened, about 1 minute. Taste and add more soy sauce, if desired. Serve.

VARIATION TIP: In place of the daikon, you can use two bunches of trimmed red radishes. If they are large, cut them in half.

Nabe

HOT POT WITH BLACK COD AND MUSHROOMS

Gluten-Free, Nut-Free, One Pot, 30 Minutes or Less

PREP TIME: 20 MINUTES | COOK TIME: 5 MINUTES | SERVES 4

The word *donabe* refers to an earthenware pot, so *nabe* has come to mean "hot pot" because of the vessel it is cooked in. I love this combination of buttery black cod, sweet napa cabbage, and the salty-tart flavor of ponzu. Typically, a portable stove is set up in the center of the table and everyone takes from and replenishes the pot as needed. I cook this on the stove and place it on a trivet when dinner's ready, then return it to the stove when more cooking is needed. Cooked rice is added at the end to make a porridge. I suggest using enoki and beech mushrooms, but wild mushrooms—like oyster, king oyster, and maitake—would also be delicious.

1 (7-inch) piece kombu

½ head napa cabbage, cut in half lengthwise, then cut crosswise into 1½-inch pieces

1 (5.25-ounce) package enoki mushrooms, trimmed and separated by hand into tiny bunches

1 (5.25-ounce) package beech mushrooms, trimmed and separated by hand

½ (14-ounce) package soft tofu, cut into 8 blocks

1 (12-ounce) package shirataki noodles, boiled for 5 minutes, then cut in half

2 leeks, white and light green parts, sliced on a diagonal into ½-inch pieces

1 (8-ounce) black cod fillet, cut into 2-inch pieces

1 cup Citrus Soy Sauce (page 26), for serving

1 recipe Basic Short-Grain Rice (page 16)

1. Pour an inch of filtered water into a large, heavy pot. Add the kombu, cover, and let sit for 20 minutes. Bring the water to a boil over medium heat.

2. Carefully arrange a couple handfuls of the napa cabbage, enoki and beech mushrooms, tofu, shirataki, leeks, and cod in a single layer in the pot, on top of the kombu. Don't try to force everything to fit; the rest will be used later. Cover the pot, turn the heat to medium-low, and cook until everything is softened, about 5 minutes.

3. Set the pot on a trivet on the table and ladle portions with just a little broth into individual bowls. Top each serving with a tablespoon or so of citrus soy sauce.

4. Keep the pot covered while everyone eats. As people take from the pot, refill it with the remaining raw ingredients, then cover the pot and return to the stove to cook.

5. When everyone has had their fill and there are only bits of vegetables and fish left in the pot, remove the kombu and add the rice. Return the pot to the stove and boil for a couple of minutes over medium heat. If there is just a little liquid, add enough hot water to the pot to make it the consistency of porridge.

6. Ladle into individual bowls and mix in a spoonful or two of citrus soy sauce.

> **VARIATION TIP:** Try a kimchi or a soy milk hot pot. **For the kimchi version:** Use thinly sliced pork belly instead of the fish, kimchi instead of the napa cabbage, and kimchi juice instead of the water. **For the soy milk version:** Replace the water with soy milk and add miso directly to the pot, a tablespoon at a time, until you can taste it. It shouldn't be salty like miso soup because you aren't having the rice until the end. You won't need the citrus soy sauce for either of these versions.

Ebi Chiri

SHRIMP WITH TOMATO-CHILI SAUCE

Gluten-Free, Nut-Free

PREP TIME: 35 MINUTES, PLUS 10 MINUTES TO REST | COOK TIME: 15 MINUTES | SERVES 4 TO 6

Chinese cuisine has long influenced Japanese food in recognizable dishes like ramen, yakisoba, and gyoza. Although lesser known, this dish is another example of Chinese influence and is easily made at home. The cooking goes relatively fast, so be sure to prepare all the ingredients before you start. Serve it on its own with rice or with Stir-Fried Napa Cabbage with Ginger (page 62) and Pork and Cabbage Pot Stickers (page 119).

---

1 pound large shrimp, peeled and deveined, tails removed

1 tablespoon baking soda

1 tablespoon potato starch or cornstarch

3 tablespoons avocado oil, divided

1 (1-inch) piece ginger, peeled and minced

1 large garlic clove, minced

1½ teaspoons doubanjiang (see Variation Tip)

½ onion, chopped

2 medium tomatoes (not Roma), finely diced

1½ teaspoons oyster sauce

Heaping ¼ teaspoon salt

1. Put the shrimp in a medium bowl and sprinkle with the baking soda. Massage the baking soda into the shrimp with your fingers, then let sit for 10 minutes.

2. Rinse the shrimp with cold water, drain well, and pat dry with a paper towel. Arrange the shrimp in one layer on a large plate and evenly sprinkle the potato starch on both sides to coat.

3. In a wok or large skillet, heat 2 tablespoons avocado oil over medium heat. Add the shrimp and cook until they release easily from the pan and the bottoms turn opaque, about 1 minute. Flip and cook for 1 more minute. Remove from the pan and set aside on a clean plate.

4. Add the remaining 1 tablespoon avocado oil to the same pan. Add the ginger, garlic, and doubanjiang and cook until fragrant, about 1 minute.

5. Add the onion and cook until softened, about 5 minutes. Add the tomatoes and cook until they break down and become like a sauce, about 5 minutes. Add water, ¼ cup at a time, if the sauce seems dry.

6. Return the shrimp to the pan and stir in the oyster sauce and salt. Cook until heated through and the sauce thickens, about 2 minutes. Serve.

> **VARIATION TIP:** Doubanjiang is a fermented paste made with soybeans and chiles. If you can't find it, you can use a mixture of miso and red pepper flakes.

Ebi Furai

PANKO FRIED SHRIMP

Nut-Free, 30 Minutes or Less

PREP TIME: 20 MINUTES | COOK TIME: 10 MINUTES | SERVES 4 TO 6

My maternal grandfather, who was a French chef, would never cook at home except to make this dish every year on New Year's Day. When my mom was little in post-war Japan, relatives would come to visit and greet each other on January first. My grandfather's ebi furai is remembered as being a special treat in those days. Now every New Year's Day in my husband's hometown of San Juan Bautista, California, a group of us cooks a feast for 80 guests, including this Panko Fried Shrimp.

½ cup all-purpose flour

2 large eggs

2 cups panko
   bread crumbs

1 pound large shrimp,
   peeled and deveined,
   tails left on

Salt

Freshly ground
   black pepper

Avocado oil or coconut
   oil, for frying

Tonkatsu Sauce
   (page 29) or tartar
   sauce, for serving

TO PREPARE THE SHRIMP:

1. Set up a dredging station by putting the flour on one large plate, beating the eggs in a medium bowl, putting the panko on a third plate, and then finally having a clean plate or tray at the end.

2. Make a series of 4 or 5 short, evenly spaced incisions along the inner curled side of the shrimp to flatten them. Rinse and drain the shrimp, then blot them dry with a paper towel.

3. Lightly season the shrimp with salt and pepper. Then, holding the tail end, douse one shrimp in the flour and shake gently to remove any excess.

4. Dip the shrimp in the egg to coat, letting any excess drip back into the bowl before placing it on the plate with panko.

5. Scoop the panko over the shrimp and press. Set the coated shrimp on the clean plate or tray while you repeat the process with the remaining shrimp.

TO COOK THE SHRIMP:

1. Heat a large cast-iron skillet over medium heat. Add ¼ to ½ inch of oil to the pan, so that it comes about halfway up the sides of the shrimp when they are added.

2. When the oil is hot (see the Oil Temperature Tests on page 11), gently lay the shrimp in the oil, being careful not to overcrowd the pan. Fry the shrimp until golden, about 2 minutes, then flip and cook until golden on the other side, 1 to 3 minutes. If your oil is too hot and the shrimp are browning before the total time, adjust and lower the heat.

3. With a slotted spoon, carefully transfer the shrimp to a plate lined with a paper towel.

4. Before frying another round of shrimp, use a fine-mesh ladle or slotted spoon to remove any panko bits floating in the oil. Add more oil if needed to make sure the shrimp will be half submerged. Let the oil heat up again, then fry the remaining shrimp and drain them on the paper towel–lined plate.

5. Serve with tonkatsu or tartar sauce.

DRY-FLAKED FISH AND AVOCADO RICE BOWL

Gluten-Free, Nut-Free, One Pot, 30 Minutes or Less

PREP TIME: 5 MINUTES | COOK TIME: 10 MINUTES | SERVES 4

I created this recipe by accident. I had sautéed canned tuna as a filling for rice balls for my stepdaughter's lunch. I was too lazy to go through the trouble of making rice balls for myself, so I filled a bowl with rice, topped it with nori, the leftover tuna, and a little mashed avocado. It was quick and surprisingly satisfying. These days, I substitute sardines for the canned tuna—I like the way they flake into smaller bits.

2 (4.25-ounce) cans boneless, skinless sardines packed in oil, drained well

1 tablespoon mirin

2 teaspoons soy sauce or tamari

2 teaspoons sake

1 recipe Basic Short-Grain Rice (page 16)

1 sheet nori, cut into thin strips

2 avocados, pitted, peeled, and mashed

Shichimi, for garnish (optional)

1. In a small nonstick skillet, fry the sardines over medium heat for about 2 minutes, breaking up the fish with a wooden spoon.

2. Add the mirin, soy sauce, and sake and continue to cook until the liquid has cooked off and you're left with dry, flaky sardines.

3. Assemble 4 serving bowls with hot rice on the bottom, then add the nori, a spoonful or two of sardines, and some avocado. Sprinkle each with a pinch of shichimi (if using) and serve.

INGREDIENT TIP: Use the flaked sardines as a mix-in when making Bonito Rice Balls (page 44).

SUSHI BOWLS

Gluten-Free, Nut-Free, 30 Minutes or Less

PREP TIME: 20 MINUTES | SERVES 4

The museum I used to work for was famous for their "sashimi lunch." A volunteer's husband would fish for tuna in the summer months and bring it in for everyone to share. A team of volunteers would come in the morning to prepare the tuna, and the rest of the staff and volunteers would bring a potluck dish to share. What a feast! Although we all can't be so lucky, here's a recipe anyone can enjoy at home.

1 recipe Basic Short-Grain Rice (page 16)

6 tablespoons Sushi Vinegar (page 27)

½ sheet nori, torn into small pieces

12 ounces sashimi-grade seafood, such as salmon, sea scallops, or tuna

4 teaspoons Dashi Soy Sauce (page 25), for garnish

2 teaspoons finely chopped scallion, for garnish

1. Put the cooked rice in a large, wide bowl. Slowly pour the vinegar evenly over the rice and mix quickly but gently, alternately using a slicing motion and scooping then flipping the rice from bottom to top. Once it looks like the grains have been coated in the vinegar, cool the rice by waving a hand fan or stiff piece of paper over the rice (see Prep Tip on page 77). Set aside to cool to room temperature. Occasionally slice, scoop, and flip the rice to allow it to cool evenly.

2. Divide the rice evenly into 4 serving bowls. Sprinkle the nori evenly over the rice.

3. Slice the sashimi on a diagonal into ¼-inch-thick pieces. If using scallops, slice them horizontally into thirds. Place the sliced sashimi evenly across the bowls, overlapping the slices if necessary to fit them all.

4. Drizzle 1 teaspoon of dashi soy sauce on each and sprinkle the scallion on top.

VARIATION TIP: To make this into a poke bowl, cube the fish and put it in a bowl with the scallion, some juice squeezed from grated ginger, dashi soy sauce, and ½ teaspoon toasted sesame oil. Add more dashi soy sauce to coat the fish, if needed. Let it marinate in the refrigerator for at least 15 minutes. Spoon onto the nori and rice and top with toasted sesame seeds. If you have it, shiso adds a bright freshness to this dish.

Temakizushi

DIY HAND ROLL SUSHI

Gluten-Free, Nut-Free, 30 Minutes or Less

PREP TIME: 30 MINUTES | SERVES 4

Is your sushi habit getting expensive? This is one of my favorite "special" meals because there's not much cooking involved and it's just a fraction of the cost of eating out. Because you're in charge, part of the fun is making up different filling combinations and discovering what you like best. When plating, consider color, shape, and type of ingredient. For example, the seafood should be to one side of the plate (or on a separate plate) and the vegetables on the other. This is great for communal eating, so invite some friends over!

The following are rough measurements. Consider the fillings you make and adjust accordingly. For example, if you have a wide array of fillings, you'll probably need less of each, and vice versa. If sashimi-grade seafood is difficult to find where you live, you could make a quick tuna salad with canned tuna, mayonnaise, and lemon juice and use that as a filling. Takuan, a yellow sweet pickled daikon radish, is also a common ingredient, usually served cut into spears. Or make it a vegetarian sushi night with Spinach Dressed with Tofu (page 48) and Miso Soup (page 20).

---

1 recipe Basic Short-Grain Rice (page 16)

6 tablespoons Sushi Vinegar (page 27)

1 Rolled Egg Omelet (page 22)

½ English cucumber or 3 Persian cucumbers, cut into 4-inch sticks

8 shiso, basil, and/or mint leaves, cut in half lengthwise

1 umeboshi, minced

1 avocado, pitted, peeled, and cut into ¼-inch pieces

1 pound sashimi-grade seafood, such as salmon, sea scallops, or shrimp, thinly sliced if necessary

2 tablespoons sesame seeds

TO SERVE

4 tablespoons soy sauce or tamari

4 tablespoons pickled ginger

1 teaspoon wasabi (optional)

8 sheets nori, cut into quarters

1. Put the cooked rice in a large, wide bowl. Slowly pour the vinegar evenly over the rice and mix quickly but gently, alternately using a slicing motion and scooping then flipping the rice from bottom to top. Once it looks like the grains have been coated in the vinegar, cool the rice by waving a hand fan or stiff piece of paper over the rice (see Prep Tip on page 77). Set aside to cool to room temperature. Occasionally slice, scoop, and flip the rice to allow it to cool evenly.

2. Lay the rolled egg omelet flat on the cutting board and slice lengthwise into thirds. Turn the sliced pieces on their side and cut in half lengthwise. Then, cut in half crosswise.

3. Arrange all your ingredients artfully on a plate or a number of plates. If not serving right away, cover and refrigerate.

4. To serve, place the nori on a small plate and arrange on the table with the rice and prepared ingredients. Provide small plates for each person.

5. To eat, take a piece of nori, spread on a thin layer of rice, and select your choice of fillings. Roll it on a diagonal into a cone. Dip in the soy sauce and enjoy!

CHAPTER SEVEN

MEAT AND POULTRY

Oyakodon

SWEET AND SAVORY CHICKEN AND EGG BOWL

Gluten-Free, Nut-Free, 30 Minutes or Less

PREP TIME: 10 MINUTES | COOK TIME: 15 MINUTES | SERVES 4

Oyako means "parent and child" and it refers to the ingredients here—the chicken and egg. The egg and sauce seep into the rice and make it jammy and delicious. This is a family-friendly dish and easy to make at home. Enjoy it with Easy Cucumber Pickles (page 35) on the side.

---

1 cup Basic Dashi (page 18)

¼ cup soy sauce or tamari

¼ cup mirin

2 boneless, skinless chicken thighs, cut into bite-size pieces

1 onion, cut into ½-inch wedges

4 large eggs, lightly beaten

1 recipe Basic Short-Grain Rice (page 16), for serving

2 scallions, green parts only, thinly sliced on a sharp diagonal, for garnish

1. In a large skillet, combine the dashi, soy sauce, and mirin and bring to a boil over medium heat.

2. Add the chicken and cook until no longer pink, about 1 minute. Add the onion wedges and cook until they are soft and the liquid has cooked down, 8 to 10 minutes.

3. Lower the heat to medium-low and pour in the beaten eggs in a slow, steady stream, starting at the center of the pan and circling outward. Let it cook until the egg is about half done, 1 to 2 minutes, then cover and cook for about 1 minute more.

4. Serve in large bowls over rice, topped with the scallions.

COOKING TIP: Traditionally, the egg is cooked so that some of it remains raw. Pasteurized eggs are safe to eat raw, and the risk of an egg being contaminated with salmonella is very low. That said, if fully cooked eggs are your preference, give it a little extra simmer time.

CLASSIC TERIYAKI CHICKEN

Freezer-Friendly, Gluten-Free, Nut-Free, 30 Minutes or Less

PREP TIME: 10 MINUTES | COOK TIME: 20 MINUTES | SERVES 3

Teriyaki chicken is a quintessential menu item at Japanese restaurants in America. I can see its appeal—the savory-sweet balance is easy to love. However, the sauce shouldn't be cloyingly sweet and thick, as I've often seen it, but just a light glaze. If you want to plan ahead, you can pop all the ingredients into a zip-top bag to marinate in the freezer. The day before you want to cook it, thaw overnight in the refrigerator. If you prefer, boneless, skinless thighs work, too.

2 tablespoons soy sauce or tamari

2 tablespoons mirin

2 tablespoons sake

1 tablespoon sugar

3 boneless, skin-on chicken thighs

2 teaspoons avocado oil

1. In a small bowl, whisk together the soy sauce, mirin, sake, and sugar until the sugar has dissolved.

2. Trim any excess fat from the chicken. Using a fork, prick the chicken all over on both sides.

3. Heat the avocado oil in a large skillet over medium heat. Place the chicken, skin-side down, in the pan and cook until the skin has browned, 3 to 4 minutes. Flip and brown the other side, another 2 to 3 minutes.

4. Transfer the chicken to a plate. Wipe the pan clean with a paper towel. With the heat still on medium, return the chicken to the pan and add the sauce. Once the sauce has come to a boil, cover the pan, reduce the heat to low, and cook for 8 minutes, flipping the chicken once about halfway through.

5. Uncover and increase the heat to medium. Baste the chicken occasionally and cook until the sauce has reduced, about 2 minutes.

6. Transfer the chicken to a cutting board and let it rest for a few minutes. When cool enough to handle, cut into ½-inch strips. Serve with a light drizzle of the pan sauce.

> **COOKING TIP:** The reason for removing the grease from the pan before cooking the chicken in the sauce is because the sauce won't stick to the meat as well with the excess oil.

PAN-TOSSED GARLICKY GREEN BEANS AND PORK

Gluten-Free, Nut-Free, 30 Minutes or Less

PREP TIME: 10 MINUTES | COOK TIME: 15 MINUTES | SERVES 4

When the days are long, be comforted by the fact that this dish will come together in the time it takes to cook the rice. Chopping the green beans can feel laborious or calming, depending on how you view cooking, but the rest comes together in a snap.

9 ounces ground pork

1 tablespoon avocado oil

12 ounces green beans, chopped

1 teaspoon sake

3 garlic cloves, minced

2 tablespoons soy sauce or tamari

1 tablespoon oyster sauce

1 recipe Basic Short-Grain Rice (page 16), for serving

1. Heat a large skillet over medium heat and cook the pork, breaking up the meat into small pieces with a wooden spoon. When no longer pink, about 2 minutes, transfer to a plate lined with a paper towel.

2. In the same pan, heat the oil and add the green beans. Toss to coat, then cook for 2 to 3 minutes, tossing occasionally. Add the sake, toss again, and let the alcohol cook off, about 2 more minutes.

3. Once the green beans begin to brown, reduce the heat to medium-low, add the garlic, and toss again. When the garlic becomes fragrant, about 1 minute, add the pork, soy sauce, and oyster sauce. Continue to toss and cook until heated through, about 2 minutes.

4. Serve over the rice.

Shōgayaki

GINGER PORK WITH GREEN CABBAGE AND RICE

Gluten-Free, Nut-Free, 30 Minutes or Less

PREP TIME: 15 MINUTES, PLUS 5 MINUTES TO MARINATE | COOK TIME: 15 MINUTES | SERVES 4

You'll be surprised at how quick and tasty this dish is. The ginger tenderizes the meat, making it melt in your mouth, but be careful not to let it sit for long—the meat will start to break down. I like to eat this with a heaping mound of sliced cabbage. The richness of the pork pairs nicely with the crunchy, fresh cabbage.

1 tablespoon peeled, grated ginger, with juice

¼ cup soy sauce or tamari

¼ cup mirin

1 pound pork loin, very thinly sliced on a diagonal

2 teaspoons avocado oil

8 loosely packed cups very thinly sliced green cabbage, for serving

1 recipe Basic Short-Grain Rice (page 16), for serving

1. In a medium bowl, combine the grated ginger, soy sauce, and mirin. Add the pork and let it marinate for 5 minutes.

2. Heat the avocado oil in a medium skillet over medium heat. Add the pork with the marinade and cook until the pork is no longer pink and the sauce has reduced, 5 to 8 minutes.

3. Serve with the cabbage on the side and a bowl of the rice.

VARIATION TIP: Although pork is traditional, you can also use beef or boneless, skinless chicken thighs.

Hambagu

HAMBURGER STEAK

Nut-Free, 30 Minutes or Less

PREP TIME: 15 MINUTES | COOK TIME: 15 MINUTES | SERVES 4

In this recipe, I find the tang of the ponzu sauce cuts through the richness of the hamburger nicely, but you can also use a mixture of half ketchup and half Tonkatsu Sauce (page 29) if you want it to taste more like a traditional meatloaf. If you go that route, no grated daikon is needed. Serve with steamed broccoli, Yoko's Sesame Dip (page 34), and Japanese Potato Salad (page 43).

---

2 tablespoons avocado oil, divided

½ medium yellow onion, chopped

½ cup panko bread crumbs

2 tablespoons milk

12 ounces ground beef

1 large egg, beaten

Heaping ½ teaspoon salt

Pinch freshly ground black pepper

Pinch ground nutmeg

1 tablespoon sake

¼ cup grated daikon

Citrus Soy Sauce (page 26), for serving

2 shiso leaves, thinly sliced, for serving (optional)

1. Heat ½ tablespoon (1½ teaspoons) avocado oil in a small skillet over medium heat. Add the onion and sauté until translucent and soft, about 5 minutes. Set aside to cool.

2. In a large bowl, combine the panko and milk. When the panko has softened, add the ground beef, cooled onion, egg, salt, pepper, and nutmeg.

3. Using your hands, mix until well combined. Divide the mixture into 4 portions and shape them into oval patties, about ½ inch thick.

4. Heat the remaining 1½ tablespoons avocado oil in a large skillet over high heat. Add the patties and cook for 1 minute, then reduce the heat to low and cook for an additional 2 minutes. Flip the patties, return the heat to high, and cook for 1 more minute. Add the sake, cover, and reduce the heat to medium-low; cook for 5 minutes.

5. Uncover and check to see if the patties are done by poking them with your finger. They should be firm and the juices should run clear.

6. Serve topped with grated daikon, citrus soy sauce, and shiso (if using).

VARIATION TIP: If you can't find shiso, an equal mix of mint and basil is a good substitute.

THE ETIQUETTE OF CHOPSTICKS

The use of chopsticks as the main eating utensil informs the material and design of the dishes in which Japanese food is served. Japanese chopsticks are made of wood, so serving dishes can be made of ceramic or lacquered wood without concerns about damaging them. This also means that served food has to be smaller in size, so it can be picked up with chopsticks, as opposed to a large piece of meat that would need to be cut with a knife and fork by the diner.

There are a few basic points of etiquette to note when using chopsticks:

- It is bad etiquette to hand someone a piece of food from chopsticks to chopsticks. Place the food item down for the other person to pick up.
- When eating a communal dish (and you're not in the company of family), use separate chopsticks from the ones you're eating with to retrieve food. Or, turn your chopsticks around and use the opposite end.
- If provided, place your chopsticks on a chopstick rest (hashioki) when you're not using them.

Soboro

GROUND CHICKEN AND SCRAMBLED EGG BOWL

Gluten-Free, Nut-Free, 30 Minutes or Less

PREP TIME: 5 MINUTES | COOK TIME: 20 MINUTES | SERVES 4

This dish comes together so fast and easy, it's often made in the morning to pack in bento lunches. The sweet chicken and egg are kid favorites, and you can pair them with simple steamed broccoli or other greens to balance out the meal.

---

1 pound ground chicken

¼ cup soy sauce or tamari

3 tablespoons mirin

2 teaspoons
 sugar, divided

4 large eggs

2 teaspoons sake

Pinch salt

½ teaspoon olive oil

1 recipe Basic Short-
 Grain Rice (page 16),
 for serving

1. Put the chicken, soy sauce, mirin, and 1 teaspoon of sugar in a large cold skillet. Turn the heat to medium and cook, breaking up the meat with a wooden spoon so the liquid is incorporated into the chicken. Cook, stirring occasionally, until the liquid has evaporated and the chicken is cooked through, about 12 minutes. Set aside.

2. In a small bowl, whisk together the eggs, remaining sugar, sake, and salt.

3. Warm the olive oil in a small nonstick skillet over medium-low heat. Add the egg mixture to the pan. Once the egg starts to cook, reduce the heat slightly and scramble slowly, using a silicone spatula to constantly move the egg around in the skillet. Cook well, about 8 minutes.

4. Divide the rice into 4 serving bowls and flatten the top gently. Cover half of each bowl with the chicken and the other with the egg and serve.

SLOW COOKER SHOYU CHICKEN

Gluten-Free, Nut-Free, One Pot

PREP TIME: 5 MINUTES | COOK TIME: 6 HOURS | SERVES 6

This is more of a Hawaiian dish than Japanese. It was adapted from one of those spiral-bound community recipe books my husband brought back on a work trip. Hawaii, at one point, was predominantly Japanese, but it was a place where many cultures commingled, resulting in interesting and distinct food traditions. Like most slow cooker recipes, this dish is low maintenance and infused with flavor.

⅓ cup sugar

½ cup tomato sauce

½ cup soy sauce or tamari

2 tablespoons rice vinegar

½ teaspoon dry mustard

1 (1-inch) piece ginger, peeled and thinly sliced

3 pounds bone-in skin-on chicken thighs

1. In the slow cooker insert, whisk together the sugar, tomato sauce, soy sauce, rice vinegar, and dry mustard. Stir in the ginger slices.

2. Add the chicken and turn to coat. Wedge the pieces in the pot so at least half of each thigh is submerged.

3. Cover and cook on low for 6 hours. Serve.

> **COOKING TIP:** For years I made this recipe on the stove. Simply bring the sauce ingredients to a boil, then reduce the heat to medium-low. Add the chicken, partially cover with a lid, and cook for 1 hour, turning the pieces over occasionally.

Nikujyaga

BRAISED POTATOES WITH BEEF

Gluten-Free, Nut-Free

PREP TIME: 20 MINUTES | COOK TIME: 30 MINUTES | SERVES 4

Simmered dishes (nimono) are exemplary of traditional Japanese cooking. They're gentle in method and the balance of flavors goes well with a bowl of hot rice. This dish doesn't have to be served hot, as the flavors are more infused when coming to room temperature. It's even better the next day.

4 Yukon Gold potatoes, peeled and cut into 1½-inch pieces

½ (12-ounce) package shirataki noodles

2 tablespoons avocado oil

10 ounces ground beef

1 large carrot, cut on a diagonal into 1-inch pieces

4½ tablespoons soy sauce or tamari, plus more if needed

2 tablespoons sake

2 tablespoons mirin

1 tablespoon sugar

1 onion, cut into 8 wedges with root intact

½ cup frozen green peas, thawed

1. Put the potatoes in a medium bowl of water to soak.

2. Meanwhile, bring a small pot of water to a boil over medium-high heat. Boil the shirataki noodles for 5 minutes, then drain. When they are cool enough to handle, cut the noodles into roughly 6-inch pieces.

3. Heat the avocado oil in a large pot over medium heat. Add the ground beef and cook until no longer pink, about 2 minutes, then transfer to a plate lined with paper towels.

4. Drain the potatoes and add them to the drippings left in the pot. Stir to coat the potatoes, then add the carrot and noodles. Cook for 2 minutes, stirring constantly.

5. Fold a paper towel into a small square and soak up the excess oil from the bottom of the pot.

6. Add the ground beef, soy sauce, sake, mirin, and sugar. Pour in just enough water to barely cover the potatoes and bring to a boil. Remove any foamy impurities with a fine-mesh ladle or spoon, being careful not to take out too much liquid along with it. Reduce the heat to medium-low and cook for 13 minutes.

7. Stir in the onion wedges and try your best to submerge them. Cover and cook for 5 minutes.

8. Uncover, turn the heat back up to medium, and continue to cook until the potatoes are tender but not quite falling apart, about 3 minutes.

9. If the onions are not cooked at this point, cover the pot and simmer until they are softened. Once the onions are soft, add the peas and let cook until warmed through. Taste and add more soy sauce, if needed. Serve.

Karaage

JAPANESE "FRIED" CHICKEN

Gluten-Free, Nut-Free

PREP TIME: 15 MINUTES | MARINATE TIME: 2 HOURS | COOK TIME: 30 MINUTES | SERVES 4 TO 6

Thanks to my friend Noelle, this baked version of Japanese fried chicken was a revelation. Not only did it taste just as good, but baking is clean, safer, quicker, and healthier than fried. A thin coating of potato starch gives the chicken a light, crisp texture. While cornstarch is often a good substitute for potato starch as a thickener, I don't recommend using it in this recipe. Serve this with plain rice or Mixed-Vegetable Sushi Rice (page 78) and Green Beans with Sesame (page 51).

¼ cup soy sauce or tamari

2 tablespoons sake

4 teaspoons sugar

4 garlic cloves, grated

2 pounds boneless, skin-on or skinless chicken thighs, trimmed and cut into 2-inch chunks

¾ cup potato starch

Lemon wedges, for serving

1. In a large bowl, whisk together the soy sauce, sake, sugar, and garlic. Add the chicken to the bowl and mix to combine. Cover and refrigerate for at least 2 hours.

2. When you're ready to bake, preheat the oven to 425°F. Line a rimmed baking sheet with parchment paper.

3. Sprinkle a generous layer of potato starch onto a large plate or shallow bowl. Add a few pieces of chicken and move them around to coat all sides. A light coat is all you need—you don't want the potato starch to be caked on.

4. Shake off any excess starch and place the chicken on the baking sheet, making sure not to crowd the pieces. Repeat with the remaining pieces of chicken, adding more potato starch to the plate as needed.

5. Bake for 20 minutes, then flip the chicken pieces. Continue baking until the chicken is golden brown, about 10 more minutes.

6. Serve with lemon wedges on the side.

> **VARIATION TIP:** Ginger is usually included in most Japanese fried chicken recipes, but I like the simplicity of just garlic. If you'd like to try it, replace 2 of the garlic cloves with 1 (1-inch) piece ginger, peeled and grated.

Gyoza

PORK AND CABBAGE POT STICKERS

Freezer-Friendly, Nut-Free

PREP TIME: 40 MINUTES | CHILL TIME: 30 MINUTES | COOK TIME: 10 MINUTES PER BATCH | SERVES 4 TO 6

You can probably guess how pot stickers got their name. Thankfully, using a non-stick pan minimizes both the frustration when cooking and the amount of work during cleanup. Pot stickers are my secret weapon because they freeze well. To freeze, place the pot stickers on a baking sheet (without them touching) and place in the freezer. Once frozen hard, transfer to a zip-top bag, squeeze out as much air as possible, and seal. When you're ready to cook them, simply place them frozen in a hot pan and proceed as instructed below. Increase the cooking time by a few minutes if cooking from frozen.

¼ small head cabbage

1 bunch scallions, white and green parts, trimmed and thinly sliced

4 garlic cloves, grated

8 ounces ground pork

2 tablespoons sake

1 tablespoon toasted sesame oil, plus more for drizzling

1 teaspoon soy sauce or tamari, plus more for serving

1 teaspoon oyster sauce

Salt

Ground white pepper, plus more for serving

1 (10-ounce) package pot sticker wrappers

1 teaspoon avocado oil

⅓ cup water, plus more as needed

Rice vinegar, for serving

> continued on next page

1. Cut the cabbage into pieces small enough to fit in a food processor. Pull apart the leaves as you place them in the processor. If your food processor is small, don't fill it more than halfway. Pulse until you have pieces about the size of a small pea. You should have a little over 2 cups. Transfer to a large bowl.

2. Add the scallions, garlic, pork, sake, sesame oil, soy sauce, oyster sauce, and a pinch each of salt and white pepper. Mix with your hands until well incorporated. Cover and refrigerate for at least 30 minutes to let the flavors meld.

3. Open the package of pot sticker wrappers and fill a small bowl with water.

4. Place a pot sticker wrapper on your palm and add a heaping teaspoon of filling to the center. Dip your finger in the water and trace the perimeter of the wrapper so it becomes wet.

5. You can simply fold it in half and press the edges together to create a tight seal. Or, starting on one side, press the edges together then make a fold, press and fold, repeating until the pot sticker is sealed. (See the Prep Tip on the next page for more about this method.)

6. Heat the avocado oil in a large skillet over medium heat for 2 minutes. Working in batches, arrange the pot stickers in the pan without touching, pour in the water, and cover. Reduce the heat to medium-low and cook for 6 minutes.

7. Uncover and poke one of the pot stickers with your finger—it should be firm. If not, cover and cook for 1 to 2 more minutes, adding more water if the pan is dry.

8. Once the pot stickers are firm, increase the heat to medium and let any remaining water cook off. While they're cooking, drizzle some sesame oil around the perimeter of the pan and tilt the pan to distribute. The sesame oil will give the pot stickers a crisp edge. Continue to cook until the pot stickers are browned on the bottoms, about 1 minute.

9. Place the pot stickers on a platter, browned side up, and serve with soy sauce, vinegar, and white pepper. Repeat with the remaining pot stickers.

PREP TIP: I recommend googling "How to fold gyoza" because it's easier to watch than it is to explain on paper. It takes practice, but don't fret too much. My six-year-old daughter has been helping me since she was four. No matter how they look, they all taste delicious!

GLOSSARY

Aeru: To dress or mix together a couple of ingredients

Ageru: To deep-fry

Bukkakeru: To pour over or splash on

Chirashizushi: To chirasu means "to sprinkle or distribute evenly." There are two regional variations on chirashizushi. The version in this book has roots in Osaka, where cooked ingredients are mixed with the sushi rice and topped with thinly sliced egg crepe. In the variation from Tokyo, sliced raw fish, vegetables, and egg omelet are placed on top of a bed of sushi rice.

Dashi: The foundational broth that is used in many dishes. It's most commonly made from bonito flakes and kombu, but it can also be made from dried shiitake mushrooms and dried baby sardines or anchovies.

Dashijōyu: Soy sauce seasoned with bonito flakes, mirin, and sake

Donabe: An earthenware pot suitable for cooking, simmering, and steaming

Furikake: A condiment sprinkled over rice. There are many different kinds, containing various combinations of seaweed, sesame, fish, dried herbs, and other seasonings.

Hitasu: To steep

Iru: A method of cooking where the pan and/or the ingredients in the pan are constantly jostled and moved around. The result should be an ingredient that is dried out or roasted and has a more intense flavor.

Itameru: To stir-fry over medium to high heat using oil

Katsuobushi: Dried bonito flakes

Maze gohan: Mixed rice

Musu: To steam

Niru/nimono: *Niru* means "to boil or simmer" and *nimono* refers to the cooking preparation of simmering, usually in a soy sauce–based sauce.

Onigiri, omusubi: Used interchangeably, *onigiri* (*nigiru* means "to squeeze") and *omusubi* (*musubu* means "to tie") refers to rice balls. Rice balls (not always shaped in a ball) are usually filled with an ingredient like fish, meat, or vegetables, or an ingredient is mixed into the rice, which is then shaped and wrapped in nori.

Otoshibuta: A drop-lid that is placed inside a pot to help cook ingredients more evenly and prevent too much liquid from evaporating

Panko: Breadcrumbs made from a soft Japanese bread called shokupan

Ponzu: A salty and tart condiment traditionally made from Japanese citrus, soy sauce, bonito flakes, and kombu

Saibashi: Long chopsticks used for cooking over the stove

Shamoji: A wooden or plastic paddle used for mixing and serving rice

Shiso: A fragrant Japanese herb (a variety of perilla) with some citrus notes

Shoyu: Japanese soy sauce made from soybeans, wheat, and koji

Suribachi, surikogi: *Suru* means "to rub." *Suribachi* refers to the vessel (mortar) and *surikogi* refers to the stick used for rubbing/grinding (pestle).

Sushi oke, hangiri: A wide, wooden tub, traditionally made from cypress, used to make sushi rice

Sushizu: The mixture of vinegar, sugar, and salt used to make sushi rice

Takikomi gohan: Rice that is cooked with seasonal ingredients

Tamagoyaki: A sweet rolled egg omelet eaten as a side dish or with sushi

Temakizushi: A type of hand-rolled sushi that doesn't require a bamboo mat to roll

Wasabi: A green Japanese horseradish most often grated and eaten with sushi, sashimi, or cold soba noodles

Yaku: To grill or bake. This is the cooking technique used to make dishes like yakitori (grilled chicken), yakiniku (Korean-style barbeque), and yakionigiri (grilled rice ball).

Yuzu: A fragrant yellow or green Japanese citrus with a bumpy surface and a flavor like a cross between a lemon and an orange

MEASUREMENT CONVERSIONS

VOLUME EQUIVALENTS (LIQUID)

US STANDARD	US STANDARD (OUNCES)	METRIC (APPROXIMATE)
2 tablespoons	1 fl. oz.	30 mL
¼ cup	2 fl. oz.	60 mL
½ cup	4 fl. oz.	120 mL
1 cup	8 fl. oz.	240 mL
1½ cups	12 fl. oz.	355 mL
2 cups or 1 pint	16 fl. oz.	475 mL
4 cups or 1 quart	32 fl. oz.	1 L
1 gallon	128 fl. oz.	4 L

OVEN TEMPERATURES

FAHRENHEIT (F)	CELSIUS (C) (APPROXIMATE)
250° F	120° C
300° F	150° C
325° F	165° C
350° F	180° C
375° F	190° C
400° F	200° C
425° F	220° C
450° F	230° C

VOLUME EQUIVALENTS (DRY)

US STANDARD	METRIC (APPROXIMATE)
⅛ teaspoon	0.5 mL
¼ teaspoon	1 mL
½ teaspoon	2 mL
¾ teaspoon	4 mL
1 teaspoon	5 mL
1 tablespoon	15 mL
¼ cup	59 mL
⅓ cup	79 mL
½ cup	118 mL
⅔ cup	156 mL
¾ cup	177 mL
1 cup	235 mL
2 cups or 1 pint	475 mL
3 cups	700 mL
4 cups or 1 quart	1 L

WEIGHT EQUIVALENTS

US STANDARD	METRIC (APPROXIMATE)
½ ounce	15 g
1 ounce	30 g
2 ounces	60 g
4 ounces	115 g
8 ounces	225 g
12 ounces	340 g
16 ounces or 1 pound	455 g

INDEX

ACKNOWLEDGMENTS

To the team at Callisto Media and especially Gleni Bartels, who patiently guided me and was my advocate. Thank you for this opportunity and trusting me with the material.

To my village, the friends who made this possible. Time, after all, is a commodity not easy to come by as a working mom. Among them are:

Noelle Singh, for encouraging me every step of the way, looking after Kiyona, meticulously testing recipes, lending her perspective on early drafts, texting me sources of inspiration, and delivering cauliflower on a moment's notice.

Anahí Parra and Anna Sochynsky, for knowing how hard it is to ask for help and making me feel completely comfortable asking for it. You guys are my EB and I've got your back, too.

Rebekah Bunya, Hanna Cassell, Debbie Fortmiller, Gena Hamamoto, Joyce Haniu, Dan Hockenson, Juli Kang, Cindi Kusuda, Naomi Lam, Mailisia Lemus, Mia Monnier, Thu-Van Nguyen, Anahí Parra, Edlín Reconco, Noelle Singh, Anna Sochynsky, Vikki Waterbury, and Hirono Yonei, for enthusiastically recipe testing. It makes me happy to know these dishes have passed through your kitchens.

Yoko Maeda Lamn, for her expertise and immeasurable source of inspiration. I'm excited for what's to come. Asaki Shinada, for looking after Kiyona, but most of all for giving me emotional support. Akko Nishio and Yoko Ward, for stepping in when I needed a little extra time.

Naomi Hirahara, for generously sharing her knowledge about the publishing world. I felt better equipped to jump in because of you. Chuong Bui, for translating the legalese.

My mom, Yoko Toyama Besch, for putting up with my kitchen messes and teaching me skills in cooking and in life. There isn't anyone I feel more synchronicity with when we cook together.

My dad, Yujiro Oda, for giving me something I took a long time to appreciate—a life in Japan. That experience made a great impact and gave me a sense of pride. Thank you.

Akira, who supports me in countless ways, is always willing to meet me halfway, and makes me laugh by saying things like "Your pot of oil is boiling." And to Kiyona, for understanding when I didn't have time to play. I hope you cook from this book one day.

ABOUT THE AUTHOR

Azusa Oda is an avid home cook, food blogger, and designer. She comes from a long line of professional and home cooks, and her abilities in the kitchen have been heavily influenced by growing up as her mother's sous chef. Raised in both Tokyo and the Bay Area of California, she had a bicultural upbringing that shaped the way she views Japanese culinary traditions and techniques.

She created her blog, HumbleBeanBlog.com, in 2008 to share her contemporary variations on Japanese dishes and to show that simple and delicious Japanese food can be made at home with relative ease. While cooking is one of her passions, she nurtures an equal interest in design and has an MFA from California College of the Arts. She lives in Los Angeles with her husband and daughter.